WHAT CAREER PROFESSIONALS HAVE TO SAY ABOUT *LAND THE JOB YOU LOVE!*

"This book should be read by anyone over 50 who is out there competing in today's job market. Mary Eileen has thoroughly covered every aspect of the job search process and provided up-to-date techniques that are certain to produce resu[illegible] difficult market."

—Carole Martin
America's #1 Interview Coach
Principal, Interview Coach.com
Interview Expert/Contributing Writer: *Mon[illegible]*
Author: *Interview Fitness Training*: *A Workou[illegible]*
Interview Coach & *Boost Your Interview IQ*

"*Land the Job You Love* gives the reader a positive perspective and a straightforward message—plus it includes all the necessary action steps. Absolutely right on target!"

—Pat Torchiana
CEO, Torchiana, Mastrov & Sapiro, Inc.
Northern California's Largest Independently Owned Career Management Firm
Member, Career Partners International

"Ms. Williams is spot-on with her comments about the need for networking, how to write a no-nonsense, attention-grabbing resume, and how to prepare for the interview (uniquely valuable were orienting the interview around the goals of the interviewer and what to bring to the interview). This book's combination of broad conceptual 'ah ha's' and fanatical attention to detail make it a 'must read' for the job seeker over 50 and a 'should read' for those of younger age. The pages are formatted for the reader to actually practice the author's suggestions and turn great ideas into successful marketing pieces for the job search. Well done!"

—Patricia Silva
Vice President, Human Resources

"As an HR professional myself, I can appreciate the time, effort, and expertise that went into this comprehensive how-to guide. There's everything here from a list of action verbs to use in a resume to sample thank you letters—finally, an all-encompassing workbook on how to find a job. Although the book is geared toward baby boomers, anyone doing a job search could use this vital information. This is the best book I've seen on the topic!"

—Judith Marshall
President, Human Resources Consulting Services

LAND THE JOB YOU LOVE!

10 Surefire Strategies for Jobseekers Over 50

A Feisty Side of Fifty™ Guide for Fabulous Living

Mary Eileen Williams, M.A., NCC

Cover Design: Pop Art Diva

ISBN-10: 1-4499-7672-7
ISBN-13: 978-1-4499-7672-9

A Few Thoughts Before We Begin...

The moment one definitely commits oneself then Providence moves, too. All sorts of things occur to help one that otherwise would not have occurred. A whole stream of events issues from the decision raising in one's favor all manner of unforeseen incidents, meetings, and material assistance, which no one would have dreamed could come their way.

Goethe

If a man advances confidently in the direction of his dreams and endeavors to live the life that he has imagined, he will meet with a success unexpected in common hours.

Henry David Thoreau

Far away—there in the sunshine are my highest aspirations. I may not reach them, but I can look up and see their beauty, believe in them, and try to follow where they lead.

Louisa May Alcott

Age is an issue of mind over matter. If you don't mind it doesn't matter!

Mark Twain

AUTHOR'S NOTE

If you're holding this book in your hands, it probably means you've kissed your half-century birthday goodbye—or are close to doing so. Chances are you're tired of beating around the bush and want information that's cutting-edge and helpful, but also brief and to the point. You may have children in college, you may be planning for your retirement, or you may just have bills to pay. In any case, you need a job and you want to move quickly.

Aside from getting back to work with as little angst as possible, who wants to put up with a job they hate—especially at our age? Midlife deepens us in many regards and we look for meaning and satisfaction in our work. There may be emergency situations, when income needs supersede fulfillment, and you'll have to take an interim job for the paycheck alone. But, if that happens, you'll want to move on as quickly as you can. (That's one positive aspect of the current work world: the lack of loyalty runs both ways!)

I'm probably best known for my popular blog and radio show "Feisty Side of Fifty" (feistysideoffifty.com). However, I also hold a Master's Degree in Career Development and am a Nationally Board Certified Career Counselor. In fact, I have twenty years of experience as a job search specialist and have worked with literally thousands of jobseekers in midlife.

Whether people initiated a career change on their own or it was forced upon them through layoffs and downsizing, looking for work can be a stressful experience. There are, however, certain proven techniques older applicants can use that will greatly enhance their success at navigating the job market of today.

My goal in writing this book is to distill the key information I've accumulated over the past two decades, break it down into easy-to-follow steps, and create a users' guide that's simple to understand and will produce real results. You'll find this book to be far more than theory and a list of "how-to" suggestions. It's actually a book/workbook; each strategy comes with insider tips and a set of action steps where you can "fill in the blanks" and clearly lay out your objectives.

A sampling of the insider job search techniques you will learn:

- How to turn your age into an advantage and demonstrate the many positive aspects and added value you'll bring to your next position
- How to stress your achievements and distinguish yourself from the competition
- How to optimize your contacts and use social media to obtain critical leads and referrals
- How to proactively target companies and meet key decision-makers
- How to network your way into the hidden job market (where the majority of jobs are found)
- How to write the strongest resume for older applicants, grab the reviewer's attention, and highlight your skills and experience
- How to create a cover letter that immediately draws the reader's interest and makes them want to meet you
- How to respond to difficult behavioral style and age-related interview questions
- How to make a dynamic first impression, ace the interview, and become *the* candidate of choice!
- And much, much more

Of course, there is a certain amount of luck inherent to landing a job, but, *if you approach the job market fortified with proven strategies designed to highlight the positive aspects of being an older applicant*, you're well ahead of the game.

Now let's get going so that you can land your next job as quickly and easily as possible!

CONTENTS

INTRODUCTION

If you're over fifty and looking for work, you probably have a slew of preconceived notions about how bad the job market is for older applicants. You are also likely to have a number of concerns and questions that need to be addressed.

In the course of my twenty years' experience as a career counselor and job search specialist, I've counseled thousands of midlife career changers and jobseekers and—believe me—I've heard it all.

Here are a few of the typical concerns that surface:

- I'm too old to be competitive in today's youth-oriented marketplace.
- I haven't updated my resume in over fifteen years and have no idea what they're looking for now.
- I realize I've got skills but I'm not sure how to name them or point out my work related accomplishments.
- I did my job and did it well, but I don't know how to market myself. In fact, I don't like tooting my own horn.
- I don't have a college degree.
- My technical skills aren't that up-to-date.
- How can I interview with someone who's in his or her thirties?

There's no doubt about it—ageism is alive and well in this country. Not so surprisingly, our generation bears some culpability in that regard. If you're over fifty, you probably remember the phrase we used to bandy about in our youth with such smug conviction: "Don't trust anyone over thirty!" We can't deny that boomers put the gap in "generation gap" back in the sixties, so ageism is far from new. In fact, Congress passed the Age Discrimination Employment Act in 1967 and the term "ageism" was coined in 1968—right around the time we boomers were smarting off to our parents about how the times were "a-changin'..." (thank you, Bob Dylan)!

Now we're reaping a bit of what we have sown and there are some downright depressing stereotypes aimed at jobseekers over fifty. Here are just a few:

Stereotypes that sting!

- We're tired, slow, and unenthusiastic
- We're not technologically savvy
- We're set in our ways and don't want to try new things
- We're too expensive
- We won't want to report to a younger boss
- We're just putting in our time until retirement

Regardless of what some people may think, there are certain key strategies you can use to highlight the positive aspects of your age and experience and make you more attractive to potential employers. In this book, I'll give you these strategies and provide you with the tools to set yourself apart as *the* candidate of choice.

I'll also address the concerns listed above, show you how you can overcome these less than flattering stereotypes, and give you the practical and proven methods to conquer any age-related obstacles you may encounter.

Your age truly is an advantage—you just need to know the very best ways to present all the positive attributes you bring, and move forward with confidence and pride in your skills and experience. But first, we'll begin by rediscovering what's important to you and reigniting your passion for your career. You're over fifty and there never was a better time to find a job you love, so let's get started!

PART I

FINDING THE JOB YOU LOVE

SETTING YOUR PRIORITIES

As the old saying goes: if you aren't clear about what you want, how can you possibly know when you've got it? Nothing could represent that tried and true statement more than a job search. People typically spend more time planning their vacations, deciding on which car to buy, or even preparing a dinner party than they take to pinpoint the elements of a job that give them the most satisfaction. We may have a general idea of what we like and want, but now it's time to get specific.

Get clear on your values. You want to be very clear about what you value in a job and which work tasks you truly enjoy. Are elements like teamwork and a sense of belonging important to you? Do you value self-expression, challenge, and contribution? Are you looking for leadership opportunities and high earning potential? Write up a list of your top six values and be crystal clear on these before you start your search. That way, when a job offer comes up, you'll have a benchmark from which you can make an educated choice to accept it or not based upon your values.

Set your priorities. You'll want to initially target your job search to meet your top priorities in a practical sense, things like:

- What is your desired salary?
- How far are you willing to commute?
- How much of your time will you devote to travel?

Know your preferred work environment and the corporate culture that suits your personality. Are you a people person who thrives on a large amount of social interaction? If so, you'll wither away in a back office with limited people contact. Do you need solitary time to generate ideas and work independently? If that's the case, you'll want to be certain you'll have periods throughout your day when you can get off by yourself to reflect and recharge. Are you a structured person who dislikes last-minute changes and constant revisions? Make certain your work environment is fairly structured, too. Otherwise you'll feel your sense of order is being threatened and you may become irritable and out of sorts.

Target your job search. Give yourself a time limit in which you pursue only those positions that meet your top criteria in a number of areas. You can write out your ideal job and call it "Target A." When you reach your time limit (e.g., 15 days), revisit your priorities and readjust them—call this "Target B." *For example: Target A—will commute 20 minutes. Target B—will commute 40 minutes*. Then set a new time limit (say, another 15 days) and, once that's reached, repeat the process and move on to Target C. That way you're not giving up on Target A (your top criteria), but you're periodically readjusting your priorities and remaining focused and flexible at the same time.

Clarity equals confidence. The least effective means of promoting yourself as a viable candidate is by acting like you'll take anything. Presenting yourself as unfocused and desperate is a giant turn-off to potential employers. They're looking for confident problem solvers to resolve issues and complete projects. The clearer you are about your own goals the more you will appear as smart, self-assured, and professional.

Of course no single job will meet all of your priorities, so remember you'll want to be focused *and* flexible. Most importantly: you don't have to "settle" for less than what you're worth or take a job you don't want. In emergency situations, when you need to accept an interim position solely for the income, do so—*but keep looking!*

By remaining true to yourself and being clear on your priorities, you'll find something that's right for you in due time. It might be a bit more difficult to look for a job while you're working, but many job search experts believe you'll be perceived as an even more valuable candidate if you're searching while you're already employed. It has to do with the "grass is greener" principle—they'll want you because someone else has got you!

SETTING YOUR PRIORITIES: ACTION STEPS

Values ~

Write up a list of your six top values. These are the ones that especially motivate you and provide you with a sense of fulfillment at work. Use the list below to get you started but don't limit yourself—identify any values that are personally and professionally rewarding to you. As you come up with your list, write out your own definition of what each of your top values means to you.

Accuracy
Action oriented work
Aesthetics
Belonging
Challenge
Competency
Contribution
Creativity
Decision-making
Detailed work
Developing people
Executive title
Financial security
Helping others
High earning potential
Influence
Intellectual status
Investigative work
Job security
Leadership
Life/work balance
Moral fulfillment
Opportunities for advancement
Outdoor/physical work
Personal/professional growth
Power
Recognition
Routine
Self-expression
Stability
Time freedom
Uphold traditional values
Work independently
Work with a team

Value 1: ________________________________

What this value means to you: ________________________________

____

____

Value 2: ______________________________

What this value means to you: ______________________________

____

____

Value 3: ______________________________

What this value means to you: ______________________________

____

____

Value 4: ______________________________

What this value means to you: ______________________________

____

____

Value 5: ______________________________

What this value means to you: ______________________________

____

____

Value 6: ___________________________________

What this value means to you: ____

____

____

Priorities ~

Now that you've determined your values (the internal rewards you get from your work), consider your work priorities in a practical sense. Take some time to write out your preferences in the following categories:

Benefits
Commute time
Company size
Compensation
Duties
Flex time/ Part time availability
Opportunities to telecommute
Overtime requirements
Travel time required
Work hours
Other:

____

____

____

____

____

____

____

____

Identify your preferred work environment.
Consider a work environment where you'll truly thrive. Think in terms of opportunities for frequent social interaction or where you'd have plenty of solitary time; where you'd enjoy a fluid, ever-changing environment or one that's structured and values routine. Perhaps you prefer an office environment or maybe you'd favor being out of doors and on the move.

____

____

____

____

____

____

____

____

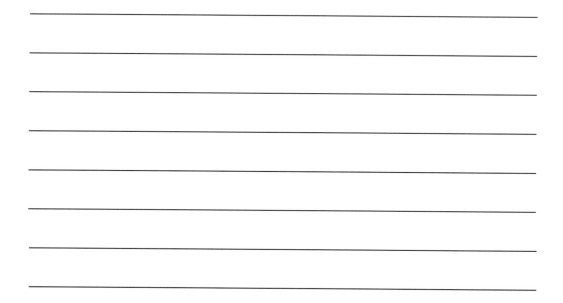

Of course, no job offer will guarantee you'll get exactly what you want in all your preferred criteria. But, by spending some time up front to determine the aspects of work that are motivating and worthwhile for you, you're much more likely to find a job you will love. When an offer comes up, revisit these pages and make certain it will provide you with most of the elements you find rewarding. This is a true win/win exercise. By finding a job you love, you're far more likely to work harder, be more successful, and bring your natural strengths and talents to the position. You'll be happy and your employers will be happy, too!

So let's get started with the #1 key that can make or break you in your search: your attitude...

FINDING WORK IS AN INSIDE JOB

Many of us will readily admit to relating to the concerns about being an older applicant and even own up to believing some of the stereotypes listed in the Introduction. As midlife jobseekers, there are legitimate reasons we've been feeling "less than" because of our age. But there's a whole lot more to the story!

Seemingly everywhere we turn, the job market is described with words such as "bleak," "slow to recover," and "with limited prospects." This, so we're told, is especially true for the older applicant. However, if you want to succeed as a jobseeker, you've got to approach your search with confidence and enthusiasm. So how can you turn those negative stereotypes around, present the positive aspects of age, and gain the confidence you'll need to mount a successful job search campaign? Let's start by taking a deep breath, getting centered, and gaining some perspective on the real truth about ageism.

Gaining a perspective on ageism

- The media knows bad news sells so that's just what they spin: *bad news* on just about everything.
- The figures they cite are drawn from generalities and take no account of the personal drive, focus, and energy an individual puts into his/her job search.
- Certain industries and occupations are far more welcoming to older applicants than others. Why not concentrate your search on fields that appreciate the knowledge that age and experience provide?
- If it looks like an employer will not appreciate the experience you bring, move on! Do *NOT* waste your valuable energy seeking possibilities that are limited at

best. Even if you are hired, they're not likely to afford you opportunities for growth. So why no place your energy on new opportunities where your experience is welcomed?
- Determine any of the potential age-related objections an employer might hold regarding you as a candidate—do something about them (if needed) and create a list of ways you can overcome these objections.
- Turn your age into an advantage.

And age truly can be an advantage! So now let's turn to just a few of the ways that you, as an older applicant, have it all over those young whippersnappers.

Your age truly is your advantage!

- You have market knowledge and a skill set gained over years of experience.
- You have an extensive network of clients, customers, coworkers, colleagues, and friends—and many of these relationships have developed over a lifetime.
- You are likely to be more flexible and can present yourself as a full or part-time employee or as a consultant.
- You are not necessarily assertively climbing the corporate ladder so you won't pose a threat to the more aggressive up-and-comers.
- You have the knowledge and ability to mentor younger workers and teach them the valuable techniques and tools that translate into ongoing success for the organization.
- You have life skills gained over years of experience dealing with people. You can get along with others, know how to manage your emotions at work, and you realize the importance of being a contributing team member.
- You have a mature work ethic. You understand the value of being responsible, showing up on time, and following through to complete assigned tasks.
- Your age has gifted you with several additional positive attributes—too many to mention in just one chapter!

The blessings of being born a boomer

If you're reading this book, it means you're either a baby boomer or close to being one. We belong to a generation known for creating sweeping and far-reaching social change. The women's movement and the civil rights movement represent just a couple of the ways we've already transformed the workforce. Better yet, we're blessed with the massive numbers to continue spearheading and succeeding with just these types of massive reforms.

Our population bulge (and, no, I'm not referring to our waistlines) has afforded us the opportunity to realize many of our generation's goals. It's true we started the youth movement back in the Swinging Sixties with our flower power, long hair, and bell-bottoms. And, now, there's no reason to think that we can't or won't start the "gray is groovy" movement and make aging the hip new thing.

In fact we already have! The workforce is graying at a rapid rate. Workers over fifty now make up about a third of the workforce and our numbers are growing exponentially. Therefore, as we represent one of the *fastest growing labor-groups in the country*, we need to appreciate the amazing strength that is produced by our numbers. Rather than allowing ourselves to feel "less than" because of our age or being discounted and pushed aside as older applicants, it's time to recognize we fit right in. We belong to the mightiest generation of them all and there are millions of workers in this country who look just like us.

Moreover, several studies have recently come to light showing, as the first wave of boomers begin to retire or cut back on work hours, there will be millions more jobs than workers to fill them. The reasoning behind these figures is the fact that there are 78 million baby boomers while the generation following us is composed of a mere 45 million.

So you do the math! The numbers speak for themselves and soon there can't help but be more jobs than workers to fill them. No longer will we be vying with our younger counterparts for positions. Organizations will recognize with even greater frequency how valuable our assets are and begin to actively woo us. Actually, given the circumstances, there has never been a better time for older applicants to find a job—*we've already changed the face of the workforce!*

Transforming the spirit and style of aging

In addition to our vast numbers, boomers have several other attributes that are hallmarks of those fortunate enough to have been born into our generation.

- We've got that "forever young" spirit and view ourselves as remaining youthful, vibrant, and active both personally and professionally. We still want to contribute and, because of that mindset, have likely kept ourselves up-to-date career-wise. Moreover, contrary to popular belief, for many of us that includes keeping up with technology.

- We're planning on working far longer than our parents—way past the traditional retirement age. We may cut back on our hours, find new and more fulfilling careers, or take on consulting work, but we enjoy the mental stimulation and income employment provides.

- We have staying power. Workers over fifty remain in positions *three times longer* than younger workers and this provides bottom-line benefits to companies. The cost of replacing experienced workers (going through the hiring process, training, and generally bringing them up to speed) can be as much as half their annual salary. So, more and more, employers are recognizing that recruiting and retaining workers over fifty is sound business practice.

- We're trailblazers known for our ability to mount sweeping social movements and create large-scale cultural change. Better yet, our numbers guarantee success. Without a doubt, there's a brand new paradigm taking hold: the days of being devalued as an older employee are drawing to a close. The culture just needs to catch up with us; it *will* change—we'll make sure of that. With our revolutionary history and trailblazing spirit, we're certainly not about to let a little thing like ageism stop us!

These are just a few of the pluses you bring as an actively engaged boomer on the move. Your attitude about your viability as a candidate and your potential for finding work underscores everything you do. Anyone seeking employment needs to project an aura of energy, enthusiasm, knowledge, and confidence. This is especially true for those of us with a few years under our belts. As we know, some of the more unkind stereotypes have us being "old," "tired," "unenthusiastic," and "technologically inept." So let's get out there and prove them wrong!

The following are some techniques for giving yourself an attitude adjustment (if needed) and keeping you motivated and on track:

The #1 rule: *It's not about how old you are... it's about how you prepare!*

Set realistic expectations. Realize you will run into a number of "no's" before your final "yes."

Recognize the roller coaster ride. A job search is not easy and you'll experience many highs and lows along the way. As much as possible, attempt to keep both your ups and downs in check. You'll need to keep your eyes on the final prize, guard your emotions, and keep plugging away.

Don't go into overwhelm. Break your projects down into achievable and realistic steps. Reward yourself on a regular basis for staying on track. Special tip: start out your day with activities you enjoy and that come easily to you. This will set the pace and keep the momentum going.

Stay organized. Set daily and weekly goals—actions you can take on a consistent basis that will move your search forward. Treat your job search as a full-time job.

Set yourself up for success. If you're lacking in certain skills (especially technical ones), take a class. Community colleges, senior centers, adult education, and several other learning institutions offer low cost classes. You will not only gain the necessary knowledge (and you can add that to your resume), you will also be able to network with your fellow students *and* the instructor. Because you are studying a subject within your targeted field, you may likely put yourself in the right place at the right time to meet influential people in your area of focus.

Keep your energy high. You'll be expending a lot of energy throughout your day and you'll need to make sure you are taking adequate care of your physical needs. Be certain to get plenty of exercise, eat right, and get sufficient sleep.

Reduce stress. After the age of fifty, you probably know the best methods you can employ to make yourself calm down and feel better after a rough day.

- Maybe you turn to friends and family for a shoulder to cry on and a pep talk.
- Perhaps you like to complete projects where you see a tangible result: cleaning out a drawer or a closet, mowing the lawn, or hanging shelves in the garage. While you're job hunting, you'll be putting out lots of effort without seeing an immediate return on your investment. Doing something with a tangible result can keep you motivated. (Keep the projects fairly small because larger ones will take your focus off your job search.)
- If you can afford a small trip, perhaps a weekend or a bit longer, you might want to take it during your search. Adding some real distance (both emotionally and physically) to an issue can often provide renewed focus and energy—not to mention what it can do for your overall attitude!

Remain flexible and open to new opportunities. You don't know where the next suggestion may lead you. Seek out every opportunity to connect with people in and outside of your field. Try new things: volunteer, join clubs and professional organizations, sign up at social networking sites, and get yourself out there.

Treat everyone you meet with courtesy and respect. Everyone with whom you come in contact is now in your personal and professional network. You always want to be viewed in a positive light and as the consummate professional.

Don't bad mouth your former employer. You may be fully justified in being angry with your former boss or company of employment. However you have to get past these negative emotions. If you need to talk your feelings out, do so only with your closest of friends and swear them to secrecy. Nothing turns people off more than dealing with someone who is angry and bitter. These sentiments will not only keep you from moving forward, they will feed negative feelings about your job search and keep your energy stuck in the past (not to mention the "red flag" you're going to raise if you make disparaging remarks during an interview).

Anticipate the transition may be difficult on a spouse or partner. Many times jobseekers feel that all the stress of the situation falls upon their shoulders alone. You need to realize, however, that spouses and others who share your household and income may also be feeling distress over the circumstances. Instead of relying solely upon your family, you might instead turn toward friends and colleagues for moral and emotional support during your search. They are not as intimately connected to your outcome and can, therefore, be more objectively encouraging of your efforts.

Remain optimistic. Recognize, even though things may be going more slowly than you'd like, that you *are* moving forward and you *will* ultimately achieve success.

Know there's lots of help out there. The Internet can be a real source of helpful information regarding the job search process and there are a number of websites springing up that cater to the older applicant. Here are a few to get you started:

- Workforce 50: http://www.workforce50.com
- Encore Careers: http://www.encore.org

- Simply Hired 50+: http://www.simplyhired.com/a/special-searches/fifty-plus
- AARP jobs: http://jobs.aarp.org
- Seniors for Hire: http://www.seniors4hire.org

Try to de-personalize the process. Many people find selling difficult—and selling themselves the most difficult process of all. But that's exactly what you'll need to do. Try to think of yourself as a product to be sold in the marketplace. You'll need to know how to position *YOU* (the product) and where *YOU* can make the greatest impact. You'll also have to distinguish *YOU* from the competition, stress your added value, and why *YOU* are the right person for the job. So get ready to define and articulate your best qualities and turn *YOU* into a best seller!

Remember, your job search is an *inside job*. Your attitude underscores everything you do—so present your strengths and abilities with confidence. You're in the prime of your life, have amassed a multitude of skills only age can provide, and you fit right in with a third of the workforce. Never allow yourself to feel "less than" or be pushed aside because of your age. After all, you are blessed with the boomer birthright: visibility, capability, and a trailblazing spirit!

With a positive attitude, energy, and confidence, you'll plug yourself right into your next job!

INSIDE JOB: ACTION STEPS

Outlook ~

Feeling a range of emotions is normal during a job search. Another gift of age is having experienced several periods of ups and downs over the years.

Which methods have you used to reduce stress in the past?

Friends and colleagues ~

People want to support you through the transition and you've likely built up a number of close relationships over your lifetime. List several people you can turn to who will pick you up on days you might be feeling low:

Activities ~

Which activities can you do to raise your energy level and keep you feeling positive? Include activities such as volunteering, exercise and participating in sports, doing things with your children, going to a movie, etc.

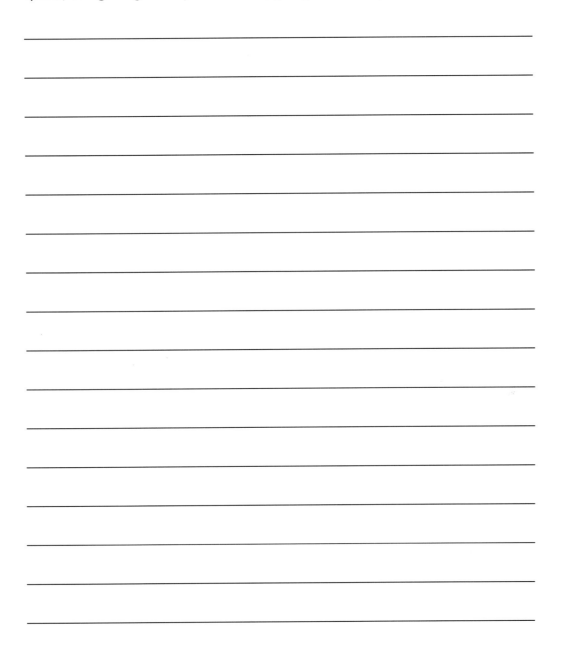

Finances ~

Worrying about finances during a job search can zap your energy and disrupt your focus. Rather than expending valuable time *worrying* about your expenses, make a list instead. Identify your necessary expenses: rent, mortgage, utilities, food, etc. Also factor in additional funds for non-essentials: clothing, transportation, recreation, etc. Then take the time to create a budget that will pull you through until you land your next position.

Essentials:

____

____

____

____

____

____

Non-essentials:

____

____

____

____

____

____

Getting organized ~

Set up a home office dedicated to your job search. You'll need to have a method to organize postings you've responded to, track with whom you've spoken and when you need to follow-up, copies of correspondence you've received and sent out, company research, daily and weekly job search goals, etc. Monitor your search by creating an online spreadsheet and/or putting together a binder.

Weekly goals: (Example: I will make 20 networking calls, send out 50 e-mails to former co-workers, spend 1 hour daily reviewing online postings.)

____

____

____

____

____

Daily goals: (Example: I will make 4 networking calls, send out 10 e-mails, spend 1 hour searching for appropriate online postings.)

____

____

____

____

____

Now it's time to move on to the surefire strategies that will help you land the job you love...

PART II

THE 10 SUREFIRE STRATEGIES TO LANDING THE JOB YOU LOVE

STRATEGY ONE: KNOW AND BE ABLE TO ARTICULATE YOUR SKILLS

As a job search consultant, I've given countless mock interviews to assist clients and candidates in preparing for the real ones. One of the most frequently asked questions in an interview is, "What do you consider to be your greatest skills/strengths?" I am constantly surprised by how many people struggle with this question. Again it goes back to the difficulties many of us have with selling ourselves. Nevertheless, if you cannot speak to your strengths and skill sets, how can you possibly land a job?

You can, however, articulate your worth and added value with a little forethought and a bit of practice. So now we're going to address that challenge and lay the process out very clearly.

There are three basic skill categories: your knowledge-based, technical skills; your personal traits and characteristics; and your transferable skills.

Your knowledge-based skills

Make a list of those skills that relate *specifically* to the work you do. For example, if you were a computer programmer, these would be skills related to programming. Think also of any special training or education you've had in your field. Come up with as many skills as you can—both those you've learned from classes and training, and those you acquired on the job.

Your personal traits and characteristics

What are the qualities that make you unique? How do you generally approach problems and deal with people? What personal talents tend to come naturally to you?

Take some time to consider the following:

- Are you a people person: friendly, cooperative, easy-going, sociable, tactful?
- Are you a leader: bold, dominant, confident, dynamic, outspoken, assertive?
- Are you a creative type: innovative, inventive, expressive, intuitive, resourceful?
- Are you someone who can diagnose and solve problems: analytical, objective, critical, astute, theoretical?
- Are you good with details, schedules, and follow-through: conscientious, orderly, efficient, thorough, organized?
- Are you physical: active, energetic, robust, vigorous?

Which personality traits would your friends identify with you? Ask them to list four or five adjectives and jot these down. In fact, ask several friends and you'll begin to see certain characteristics listed again and again.

Think of how you act when you're being your "natural" self. How were you as a child? Which personality traits have always been part of your internal makeup?

As you spend time gathering information, you'll begin to get a sense of those characteristics that set you apart from others. Finally, determine five to ten adjectives that best describe your personality and know them well.

Your transferable skills

Transferable skills transfer from one arena to another and are wide ranging. They run the gamut from budgeting and calculating to motivating and negotiating.

Transferable skills generally fall under these categories:

- People/helping skills: teaching, guiding, listening, acting as a liaison, counseling, sympathizing
- People management/persuasion skills: advising, leading, negotiating, selling, motivating, delegating

- Creative/artistic/design skills: writing, acting, decorating, designing, brainstorming, improvising, conceptualizing
- Math/science/theoretical skills: investigating, synthesizing, diagnosing, observing, theorizing
- Organizational/data/detail skills: monitoring, coordinating, scheduling, expediting, budgeting
- Outdoor/mechanical/action-oriented skills: using eye-hand dexterity, assembling, building, repairing, fabricating

Identify two or three of the categories above where your abilities lie and write out a list of skills under each.

Important point

When identifying transferable skills, only list those you *enjoy* using—those that make you feel good and give you energy as you perform them. Career counselors call these "motivated skills" because they inspire your best work and make you feel fulfilled. In fact, people often report they enter a state psychologists term "flow." They become so immersed in the task at hand, they lose track of time until they notice several hours have passed—all spent in pleasurable activity.

Remember you are selling yourself with your skills and you don't want to describe yourself as a skilled expert (even though you may be one) in something you don't like doing. That's a surefire recipe for landing a job you hate or, at a minimum, certainly a job you *do not love*!

Revisit your preferred work environment

Not only do your motivated skills point to rewarding work, they also indicate which types of work environments will suit you best. After you've identified your motivated skills, go back to Chapter 1 and take a look at the exercise you filled out regarding your preferred work environment. Do your results match up with the skill sets you've indentified as motivators for you?

- If you're a people person (your motivated skills fall under the areas of people/helping or management/persuasion), you'll probably need plenty of social interaction or your energy will flag.
- If your skills tend to be creative or theoretical (the two idea

areas), you'll likely want a great amount of free time for reflection and idea generation so you can flesh out your thoughts undisturbed.

- For those who enjoy organizational skills and working with details, you'll want a fairly structured environment where there aren't a lot of last minute changes to throw you off your schedule.
- And, if you value activity and using physical skills, you'll likely find an office environment stifling because you need plenty of opportunity to get outside and be ready for action.

Summing up your skills

This is the time to put modesty aside. Your skills represent your core competencies, unique value, and individual strengths. Take the effort to identify them and have them on the ready so that they'll roll off your tongue. You will be well rewarded for this exercise, as more times than you can count, you'll be asked to list what you can and will bring to the job.

If you're not comfortable with this process, sit or stand in front of a mirror, look yourself in the eye, and practice. You'll be amazed at how effective this technique is and how much it will help you to articulate your skills with confidence.

Furthermore, make sure your skills are visible and strongly stated on your resume and be ready to provide substantiating examples of these strengths in your interview.

Now that *YOU* are a product, your skills are what sell you to prospective buyers—in other words, potential employers. And speaking to skills is even more important for older jobseekers. We tend to stress experience. However, if you find yourself interviewing with a thirty-five year old and you keep referring to your twenty-five plus years of experience, it wouldn't be a stretch to consider he or she is likely thinking: *"old-timer!"* Employers want someone who can handle and resolve their issues and problems *now*, so sell your skills—they'll work for you every time!

STRATEGY ONE: ACTION STEPS

Knowledge-based skills ~

Make a list of skills that relate *specifically* to the work you do.

____

____

____

____

____

____

____

____

Personal traits and characteristics ~

Identify two or three areas where your personal strengths lie: helping people, leading and persuading others, using creativity, analytical and problem solving skills, coordinating and following up with details, or being physically active. Then list your strengths that fall under each of these categories.

Areas:

____

____

____

Skills:

____

____

____

____

____

____

____

____

____

____

Transferable skills ~

Remember that transferable skills are those that transfer from one arena to another. They fall under these categories: people/helping, people/leading, creative/design, analytical, detailed work, and mechanical/physical skills. Identify your top three areas of interest and then list your strongest skills under each category. Remember to list *only* those skills you enjoy using.

Areas:

____

____

____

Skills:

____

____

____

____

____

____

____

____

____

____

____

Now let's put your skills into action…

STRATEGY TWO: TURN YOUR SKILLS INTO WINNING EXAMPLES

It's time to flesh out your skill sets, demonstrate how you have put them to best use, and turbocharge marketing *YOU* (the product). Every employer is looking for the same thing—a problem solver. By fleshing out examples of how you've solved problems in the past, you're well on your way to making the sale and putting yourself back in the ranks of the gainfully employed.

Examples are important for several reasons:

- Past performance is considered the best predictor of future performance.
- People tend to remember stories over facts and data, and your examples will act as "stories" that illustrate what you are capable of achieving.
- By putting examples on your resume, you will give potential employers a look at how you go about working with others, developing ideas, handling pressure, meeting deadlines, increasing sales, etc.
- By using examples to underscore your skills during an interview, you'll prove (as much as is possible within the limits of a conversation) your knowledge, personal strengths, and skill sets.

There are basically three components to creating clear examples:

- Start with a project/challenge/problem/situation you dealt with.
- Identify the specific steps and skills you used to resolve or remedy the challenge/problem/situation.

- End with the positive result you achieved and, whenever you can, quantify (describe with numbers or percentages) your results to further flesh out what you've accomplished.

A personal example

I had a very angry and frightened client who had unexpectedly been laid off from a job she'd held for twenty-five years. She had no idea of how to go about conducting a job search and came to me for answers. However, rather than listening to my suggestions, she only wanted to vent her frustration and anger at her former employer. I was able to diffuse the situation by listening attentively, asking questions that helped her to understand and work through her emotions, giving her the practical tools to mount a successful job search, and motivating her to move forward with confidence. The result was that she landed a new job (which she actually preferred to her former work) within a period of two months.

The components of my example:

1. My project/challenge/problem/situation: distressed client who needed to find work but was stuck because of her anger and fear.
2. The specific skills I used: active listening, asking the right questions, and providing job search tools and strategies that worked.
3. The positive result I achieved underscored with a number: My client found work within two months.

Now it's your turn!

- Consider the skills you identified in each of the skill areas: specific knowledge-based skills, personal traits and characteristics, and transferable skills.
- Think in terms of skills you feel energized using—as you recall, career counselors call these "motivated skills."
- Then come up with a minimum of ten winning examples of how you've used these skills in work situations.

As you're coming up with your examples try to think of times when you:

- Saved your employer time or money
- Turned around a difficult customer or client
- Streamlined procedures and made things more efficient
- Took charge and showed leadership during a crisis
- Thought up a creative resolution to a problem
- Led a team that completed the project on time and within budget
- Found a need and filled it

It's useful to ask yourself "so what" after every example you write. This technique will help you direct the focus to the positive results you achieved—*making you appear all the more valuable to potential buyers.*

Make sure these example statements are peppered throughout your resume and that you can speak to them during an interview. By naming your skills and substantiating them with actual examples, you're providing a real-world illustration of what you are capable of achieving. Employers believe: if you've done it before, you're likely to do it again. So examples are the very best method to highlight all of your wonderful skills and experience in ways that make your actions speak for themselves.

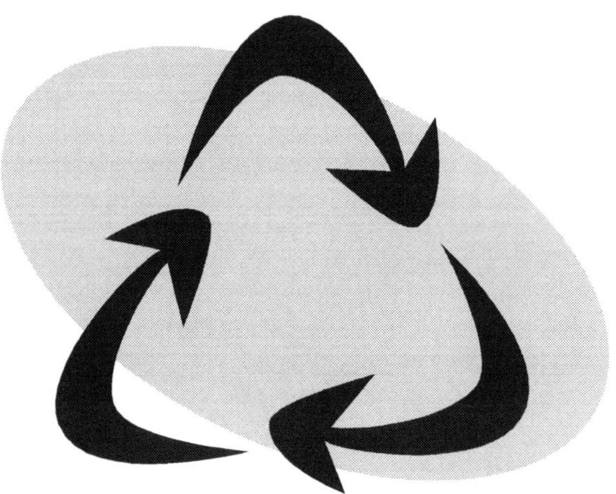

If you did it before, you can do it again!

STRATEGY TWO: ACTION STEPS

Your winning examples ~
Come up with 10 projects/challenges/problems or situations you dealt with in the past. Look for examples when you were especially engaged in the process, were proud of the outcome you achieved, and where you made a difference to your team, employer, client, or customer. Identify the specific skills you used and how your result made a difference. Quantify your results whenever possible.

Example 1

____

____

____

____

____

____

____

____

Example 2

____

____

____

Example 3

Example 4

Example 5

Example 6

Example 7

Example 8

Example 9

Example 10

Now it's time to identify your key selling points by researching and pinpointing what your customers are looking for...

STRATEGY THREE: ASSESS THE MARKETPLACE

Now that you've determined the work you love, identified your key skills and core competencies, and substantiated them with examples, it's time to assess the marketplace. Any savvy marketer knows, prior to creating and launching a product, you have to determine the needs and preferences of your potential customers—and that takes information and research.

As a jobseeker, you'll want to conduct your research on three levels:

Career Fields and Industries

- What are the most recent developments in your field: locally, nationally, and internationally? (Today's economy is a global one and you'll need to keep up so you can speak with confidence and knowledge about the latest trends.)
- What is the current demand and future growth? (Is your field expanding or contracting? There are jobs to be found within contracting industries, but you'll want to be aware of that fact so you can make an educated choice as to whether or not you wish to remain in the field.)
- What is the occupational range and opportunities for advancement within the industry? (How do these fit with your own career aspirations?)

Employers/Companies

- How large is the company and are they currently hiring?
- What is the range of occupations within the organization and how would your career path fit?
- How profitable is the firm now and what is the financial outlook?

- What are values, mission, and overall corporate culture of the organization? (This is an important piece that is often overlooked. I've counseled many jobseekers who've said they hated their jobs. It turned out it wasn't the work they disliked; it was the environment and culture that wasn't a fit. So be certain to find out as much as possible about this critical component to career satisfaction.)
- Any recent changes in management, new locations, etc. These are all indicators of potential opportunities for you.

Occupations (especially if you're a potential career changer)

- What are the general duties and responsibilities of the position?
- What additional education or training might you need?
- What is the current labor demand and future outlook for the occupation?
- What level of salary and compensation might you expect?
- Which firms might employ someone like you in the position and how would these organizations fit with the work priorities you've identified for yourself?

Research can be conducted using three main methods

Print media: Many jobseekers discount the benefit of using print media to research potential openings because the Internet has made information so easy to obtain. However, there are several valuable insights to be gained by reading the business section of your local newspapers. Read articles with an eye to management changes, company relocation, industry and organizational growth, and other key factors that may lead to job openings.

For example, if you spot an executive who has relocated to another firm, chances are she/he will want to clean house and create a new team. This could open up real possibilities for you—if you're the first one to make your presence known, you may have little, if any, competition. Also, check out the organization where she/he was formerly employed. There are likely to be opportunities there as well.

I generally don't recommend submitting unsolicited resumes, but these cases are the exception. If you write a compelling e-mail/letter of approach, mention the article and how your background is a perfect match to compliment the new team created by the move, and get your resume in the right hands, you may well be called in for an interview.

In addition to newspapers, industry magazines, professional journals, and annual reports all have worthwhile information for jobseekers.

Online sources: As we know, there are valuable articles and resources to be found on the Internet, including company websites. Most jobseekers spend the majority of their time on the postings—often for the wrong reasons. It's estimated that fewer than 15 percent of positions are obtained by responding to postings. This means you should only spend about 15 percent of your time in that activity (way less than most jobseekers). However postings can prove extremely helpful research tools: they tell you who's hiring, the skills that are currently in demand, the latest buzzwords for your industry, etc.

Research on specific companies is especially easy to uncover. Simply Google "conducting company research" and you will find a slew of great sites. Here are several to get you started:

http://www.hoovers.com
http://www.vault.com/wps/portal/usa/companies
http://www.glassdoor.com/index.htm
http://www.quintcareers.com/researching_companies_guide.html
http://jobsearch.about.com/cs/employerresearch/a/companyresearch.htm

You can also find local companies in your field by using quotation marks to specify industry and location and entering this into your favorite search engine. For example: "software companies in Boston." Then enter the same information without using quotation marks—you may come up with even more resources.

Word of mouth: This is one of the best ways to conduct research. You're not only getting information—the information is current, from an insider's point of view, and you're networking at the same time. It's a win/win/win situation!

Social networking sites like LinkeIn will prove especially useful here. After you've identified companies in which you have an interest, go through your contacts and see if you can find links to people who work for these organizations or who may know of people who do. (We'll be going over the best and most effective methods to using this networking technique in Strategy Six.)

Indentify your key selling points

You have already pinpointed your motivated skills; now it's time to present them in such a way that the market will buy *YOU* (the product). Through your research, identify the skills that come up again and again (as requested in ads and postings). Then match your core competencies (key skills) to what they're looking to "buy." Get specific and make a list—and be certain to use the latest terminology. You'll need to appear knowledgeable, competent, and current.

Remember, most employers are going to be less impressed by your level of experience and swayed more by the skills you bring supported by your past accomplishments. By identifying and stressing these key selling points on your resume, while you're networking, and during an interview, you'll be well on your way to landing your next position.

Save yourself time and effort with a little upfront research!

STRATEGY THREE: ACTION STEPS

Remember to use each of the three information sources as you conduct research on:

Industries ~

Latest developments and trends (locally, nationally, internationally):

____

____

____

____

____

____

____

____

Current demand and projected future growth—is your field expanding or contracting?

____

____

____

Occupational range and potential career implications:

____

____

____

____

____

____

____

____

Companies ~

Company size, potential growth, and current hiring trends:

____

____

____

____

____

____

____

Existing profitability and projected financial outlook:

____

____

____

____

____

____

Overall corporate culture:

____

____

____

____

____

Management and organizational changes:

____

____

____

____

____

____

Occupations~

General duties and responsibilities of the position:

____

____

____

____

____

____

Additional education and training you might need:

____

____

____

____

____

Current labor demand, future outlook, expected compensation level:

Potential employers who would hire for this occupation:

Your key selling points presented in today's terminology:

____

____

____

____

____

____

____

____

____

____

____

____

____

____

____

Now that you've done your due diligence, let's turn your skills and examples into a marketing brochure that's guaranteed to open the door to a job you will love...

STRATEGY FOUR: OPEN THE DOOR WITH A RESUME THAT ROCKS!

Before you begin actively marketing *YOU*, you'll need two things: a catchy commercial and a product brochure (aka resume). Why? Because the first thing someone will ask you is, "what do you do?" and you'll want to have a verbal message prepared that presents your background in a positive and memorable light. Secondly, should they want to help you, they'll likely ask for your resume.

We'll start with your resume because, by identifying your core skills and accomplishments and committing them to paper, you'll gather your thoughts and prioritize the key selling points for your catchy commercial. These are both critical components to your job search. In fact, you're about to brand *YOU!*

What are the main reasons for a resume?

- It's the marketing brochure that defines *YOU* (the product), your skills and experience, and how you differ from the competition.
- It's the tool to convince potential "buyers" that you have the right stuff to do the job. Interviews are generally more about attitude and fit, but resumes are more about skill sets and experience.
- It gets you through the door to the interview by arousing the readers' interest and making them want to see you!

There are three basic types of resumes

Chronological: Work experience is listed by date with the most recent positions at the top of the resume—in other words, in reverse chronological order.

Functional: Work experience is displayed with winning examples at the top of the resume—often listed under skill headings, e.g., "Marketing," "Management," and "Sales." Position titles and places of employment are shown at the bottom.

Combination/hybrid: Just what it says—this type of resume includes elements of both the chronological and functional styles. The combination resume is generally the most successful format for the older, more experienced worker.

(For examples of all three styles, simply list each type in your favorite search engine and check them out online, e.g. "sample chronological resume.")

We're going to spend our time focusing on the combination resume for the reason stated above. However, before we begin with the rules of formatting, there are some basic guidelines to address and a few new aspects to resumes that were never considered twenty years ago. You know your resume must be error free, but did you know that...

A winning resume is—

Brief and to the point. Use enough material, however, to cover the important aspects of your work history. Forget about the old rule of a one-page resume. Trying to cram significant experience onto a single page is not doing you any favors. Nevertheless, everything of greatest relevance and importance *must* appear on the first page so that a reviewer will immediately see your strengths and your fit with the position. You only need to focus on the most recent ten to fifteen years of experience. Remember a resume is not a life history. Rather it is a tool to arouse interest and "open the door."

Make it current. Highlight skills that are in demand now, not twenty years ago. Search postings and ads to find the latest buzzwords in your industry. Chances are you already have the skills; you just need to be sure to describe them in today's terms. For example, what was called "personnel management" years ago would now be referred to as "human resources management," "talent development," or "performance appraisal monitoring."

Pay particular attention to key skills you see over and over. Make certain (if they're true for you) that these skill words appear throughout your resume.

Make it "eye friendly." Use a good-sized font that's easy to read with liberal use of white space and bullets to set off your key skills and examples. Realize that most reviewers will have a stack of resumes on their desk (or the digital equivalent on their computers) and will probably spend no longer than 30-seconds determining if your resume is worth reading. Thus you'll *need* to make the information literally leap off the page.

Do *NOT* use paragraphs to describe your prior work experience. There is no way to find and identify key skills quickly within dense blocks of text. Rather, be *SURE* and use bulleted statements that draw the eye.

Make certain your resume can be easily scanned. Even if a reviewer decides to read through your resume, she/he will probably only scan it the first time through. Key skills and experience must be placed in a certain order. In English, we read from top to bottom and from left to right. That means you must list skills and bulleted statements with the most relevant and important items placed to the top and to the left.

Write in memo style not prose. Resumes include short examples of you performing your work at its best—not full sentences. Most often the subject is omitted and the statement begins with a past tense verb. Also, eliminate the use of any personal pronouns such as "I" did this, "she" did that, or "they" did whatever.

Your resume highlights your achievements. Emphasize your winning examples rather than your job duties. Relying solely upon the terms, "responsible for" and "duties included," so prevalent on resumes of the past, is now regarded as passé. Basically "responsible for" and "duties included" are position descriptions—they do not describe what you actually accomplished.

In today's highly competitive market, you'll need to more actively represent your work experience. So stress those challenges you faced, the skills you used to overcome them, and the positive results you achieved. Remember that past performance is considered the best predictor of future performance—that's why your examples are so critical to landing the job. However, you can use "responsible for" to provide a brief job description if you think it will serve you.

Make it compelling. Develop compelling stories that connect with your goals. Ask yourself the following: Does your resume sell you to the reader? Are you communicating meaningful information that convinces others you can be successful at a specific job in a particular industry?

Customize, customize, customize! Like "location, location, location" are the buzzwords for real estate, fit is the essential element for landing a job. "One resume suits all" is no longer possible with today's technology. In many instances, you'll be responding to postings online. Unless the scanning software picks up your resume (because the skills it has been programmed to identify are readily apparent), your product brochure will never be seen. Sadly, without the required skills clearly stated and easily scanned, your resume is destined for the fathomless, black hole of cyberspace—it will fade away, unseen by the human eye.

The same is true for smaller companies that may not advertise online. The screener (this time a person) will be given a stack of resumes and asked to look for key skills. Rarely is a first-level screening done by hiring managers—usually the screener is an assistant or a human resources specialist who may have little actual knowledge of what the job entails. This means they cannot make assumptions as to your skills unless they are explicitly stated. If the sought after skills are not listed at the top of the resume and "eye friendly" so that they are easy to find, your resume will land in the black hole of the trashcan.

That's why customization is so important. You'll want to create a basic resume, use it as your template, and then take it from there and *customize*. It's far better to send out five targeted resumes than fifty that are boilerplate.

But now for the big question!
How do you know which skills to highlight? Well, the answer isn't all that difficult: *They tell you!* Remember employers are buying *YOU* and what you can do for them. As the "buyer," they provide a detailed description of what they want. The skills and experience they're looking for are listed in the posting or newspaper ad.

Of course your resume needs to be honest, but your job is to give employers what they're asking for, so match your skill set with their needs as closely as possible. This is not the time to get creative! Give them what they want and highlight your skills and experience in basically the same order they've listed the requirements in their ad. And don't forget to use the current terminology. You want to present yourself as a skilled, up-to-date, expert in your field.

Employers have projects that need completion and problems that need to be solved. They're looking for the right person for the job. By matching your skills to what they need, you're already halfway there.

A resume is a future-oriented document
We generally think of resumes as written records of our work history. However, if you flip your thinking to assign your resume a future-oriented focus, you'll learn to highlight the skills you enjoy using (your motivated skills) and back these up with examples of your best work. Whatever you put down on your resume must be truthful. However, it is *your choice* where you place your emphasis. So take some time to identify opportunities you think you'll enjoy, focus your resume in that direction, and you'll be heading straight for a job *you will love*!

Get feedback
Ask coworkers and friends you trust to give you their take on your resume, but realize their suggestions may not always be the right ones for you. Remember, nothing is set in stone and resumes are constantly changing anyway—so ask for feedback but always trust your gut.

The 30-second test—
A good way to find out what reviewers might see and remember about your resume is to give your friends the 30-second test. Ask them to review your resume while you silently count to thirty. At that point, request they hand your resume back to you. Then ask them what they remember. This is a real-world example of how effectively you're getting your information across.

Another real-world example of how effective your resume is performing comes from an even more reliable source. Are you getting responses when you submit your resume? If not, it needs additional work.

Format for the combination/hybrid resume

Even though the most important pieces of information must appear on page one, it's easiest to begin the process of writing your resume on page two—at the back and at the bottom. So let's start out with the very final section and work our way from back to front.

The final section
The last section of your resume should be about your education. (There are a number of resume examples that put education at the top of page one. That is fine for very young applicants who are recent college graduates because, by placing education there, they are highlighting this as their most important feature. For older candidates, unless the position specifically requires listing your education at the top of your resume, this is inappropriate. Instead, you'll want to highlight all of your fabulous skills and experience.)

If you have a college degree(s), you will list it (them) like this:

EDUCATION

M.A., Psychology, University of California, Berkeley, California
B.A., Communications, California State University, San Diego, California

Tips:

- The most recent degree goes at the top.
- You do not need to list the year you graduated.
- If your degree is in an area that has little or nothing to do with your current field, you don't have to name it. Only write the actual degree such as "B.A." or "B.S."

If you've taken additional formal or on-the-job training, have a separate section under your education entitled ONGOING PROFESSIONAL DEVELOPMENT. (Or you can combine the two under the heading EDUCATION AND ONGOING PROFESSIONAL DEVELOPMENT.) The wording is important because "ongoing" suggests a desire for lifelong learning—something employers like. Also "professional development" says it all. Then beneath that heading, list any classes you wish to highlight.

If you do not have a college degree, *do not omit* this section—it will immediately draw attention due to its absence. Simply substitute the "ONGOING PROFESSIONAL DEVELOPMENT" section and list your training there.

Here's an example:

ONGOING PROFESSIONAL DEVELOPMENT

Seminar presentation training

Sales training for consumer products

Professional selling skills courses

MS Office (Word, Excel and PowerPoint)

The body of your resume

The bulk of your resume will center on where you've worked, the dates of your employment, your job title, and example statements of you performing your work at its best. There is a specific style to laying this out in an easy-to-read fashion.

Here's how you do it:

XYZ COMPANY, Albany, New York 2001- 2009
Director of Marketing

- Example Statement #1
- Example Statement #2
- Example Statement #3
- Example Statement #4
- Example Statement #5

ABC COMPANY, Trenton, New Jersey 1997 - 2001
Marketing Manager
Responsible for creating all marketing programs and collateral materials.

- Example Statement #1
- Example Statement #2
- Example Statement #3

Tips:

- Notice employment dates are to the right. These are far less important than where you worked and your job title. (Remember, everything of importance goes toward the top and the left.)
- There are more examples listed under the most recent position. You want to highlight and flesh out your most recent experience whenever possible.
- There is a brief "responsibility statement" under ABC Company. Here is where you can put a short position description using terms like "responsible for" and "duties included" if you believe it will serve you. However, unlike our example and to make your resume consistent, if you write a position description for one job, you'll want to add a description to all of the positions you've listed on the first page.

How to write an example statement:
First, let's recall the elements of a winning example—

1. Start with a project/challenge/problem/situation you dealt with.
2. Identify the specific steps and skills you used to resolve or remedy the challenge/problem/situation.
3. End with the positive result you achieved and, whenever you can, quantify (describe with numbers or percentages) your results to further flesh out what you accomplished.

Now let's return to my personal example. If you recall, I had a difficult client who was stuck in her anger and fear. So I used my listening and questioning skills to help her move through her emotions, provided her with successful job search strategies, and helped her regain her confidence. As a result, she landed a new position within two months.

We're now going to turn this into an example statement alá "resume mode." Remember, we're eliminating personal pronouns, we're writing in memo style, and we're leaving off the subject—in this case, me. We're also beginning with a past tense verb that resume writers call an "action verb." Action verbs form the very heart of your resume because they show ownership of a skill set; you've done it before so you can do it again!

This is how my example will look on my resume:

- Utilized counseling skills as well as proven job search techniques to actively support client in successfully obtaining a new position within two months.

Let's look at another example statement—this one is from a salesperson's resume:

- Followed through with all leads and provided excellent account services, thereby exceeding sales quotas and increasing sales at key account level by 30%.

Looks good, doesn't it? But our friend, the salesperson, could make her example even stronger and more impressive. Remember that anything of importance should go towards the top and the left. Well, that also includes example statements. In this case, if the salesperson put her results (exceeding sales quotas and increasing sales at key account level by 30%) at the beginning of the example rather than at the end, she would certainly attract more attention.

So let's revisit this one more time:

- Exceeded sales quotas and increased sales at key account level 30% by diligently following up on all leads and providing excellent account services.

Now how great is that? The reason this eye-catching statement is so strong is explained by the principles of marketing. And, as you know, you're marketing *YOU* with your resume. The two main terms in marketing are "features" and "benefits." To describe how these work, let's think back to a commercial any of us over fifty will remember:

Bryl-creem, a little dab'll do ya,
Use more, only if you dare,
But watch out,
The gals will all pursue ya—
They'll love to run their fingers through your hair.

The *features* of this fine product are the fact that it kept men's hair in place and gave it a bit of shine as well. But there's absolutely no mention of that in the jingle. Why? Because people buy on what they believe a product will do for them—the *benefits*. In the case of Brylcreem, the idea of women clamoring to run their fingers through a head of hair plastered with goo was enough to keep sales skyrocketing.

You'll need to state both your features and benefits on your resume. Your skill sets are your features, but the positive results you achieved are the benefits an organization will expect to reap when they "buy" *YOU*. So always, always, always stress those benefits—they'll sell you every time!

Here is more from the salesperson's resume:

HOTSHOT SALES, Austin, Texas 1998 – 2003
Sales Representative

- Ranked as one of the company's top five account managers by consistently exceeding monthly and annual goals.
- Increased product line sales by 20% through conducting end-user calls and consumer seminars.
- Provided total customer satisfaction by professionally responding to needs of over 300 accounts: ensured order accuracy and identified future needs.

(Notice that the results are displayed *at the left of the example*. This is the strongest example statement you can write. Although your resume will be scanned, you'll be sure to draw the eye and the attention of the reviewer by putting your results to the left.)

Now it's your turn!
Take the examples you've already created and turn them into bulleted statements for your resume. For help and inspiration, just go to your favorite search engine and type in "action verbs." There are great lists to be found online that should get your little gray cells revved up and working—and don't forget to quantify and highlight your results whenever possible. Here's a site that lists action verbs under skill sets—very helpful!
http://www.quintcareers.com/action_skills.html
(A list of action verbs and words that highlight results are also listed at the end of this chapter.)

A point about numbers
Many careers do not lend themselves to using numbers to quantify results. In this case, you can set off your example statements and results by using words such as, "enhanced," "exceeded," "improved," "maximized," "revitalized," etc.

And one more time: for an added blast of success—*put your results to the left!*

Get your computer humming with keywords, examples, and results that will translate to your success!

The combination/hybrid resume—a boon to older applicants

Now we're coming to a very exciting part of the combination resume. You know that everything of importance, and that will distinguish you from other candidates, should go to the top of your resume. The most impressive experience must be presented in an "eye friendly" manner so that it can readily be found within a 30-second scan. But, for many older applicants, some of their strongest example statements may be found under positions that were not their most recent. Therefore, they may be languishing, unseen, way back on page two.

Voila! Unlike the chronological resume, the combination resume has a special section at the top. You can term it "Selected Accomplishments," "Career Highlights," "Significant Contributions," or something along those lines. Here is where you draw from your *entire* career and work experience, and place your strongest, most impressive example statements where they'll be sure to grab the attention of the reader.

Let's take a look at our salesperson's resume (an abbreviated version) once again and see what we've got so far:

SELECTED ACCOMPLISHMENTS

- Achieved 40% increase in annual sales by spearheading and administering strategic marketing and advertising campaign.
- Accomplished double-digit sales within first year in new accounts position and expanded territory to $6 million plus in annual sales.
- Recognized for four consecutive years as "Salesperson of the Year" at XYZ Company, outperforming 200 other vendors.

PROFESSIONAL EXPERIENCE

GET IT CHEAP, Tremont, New Jersey 2003 – Present
Account Manager/Sales Representative

- Exceeded annual sales objectives by 25% due to sound sales acumen and active prospecting.
- Cultivated business relationships with over 250 new clients in the United States, Mexico, and Canada, within a 12-month period.
- Launched product promotions, establishing successful business relations in printing, publishing, and media markets.
- Increased customer retention levels by 15% within highly competitive markets by providing excellent customer service.

HOTSHOT SALES, Austin, Texas 1998 – 2003
Sales Representative

- Ranked as one of the company's top five account managers by consistently exceeding monthly and annual goals.
- Increased product line sales by 20% through conducting end-user calls and consumer seminars.
- Provided total customer satisfaction by professionally responding to needs of over 300 accounts: ensured order accuracy and identified future needs.

ONGOING PROFESSIONAL DEVELOPMENT

Seminar presentation training

Sales training for consumer products

Professional selling skills courses

MS Office (Word, Excel and PowerPoint)

Your professional profile

Here's where you'll introduce yourself and display your top skill sets. Remember a resume is often a first impression of *YOU* so this is where you can really wow them! It's generally the first item the reviewer will see, and it goes at the very top of your resume—just under your name and contact information.

You don't need an objective statement because the profile begins with your position title in bold—it's easy to determine what you're going for. Your profile should consist of a statement of your experience, key transferable and knowledge-based skills, and, if you choose, some personal/professional strengths as well. (You'll notice the last sentence in the profile below states: "Easily establishes rapport and builds strong customer relations.")

Here's our salesperson's professional profile:

Sales Management Professional with 20 plus years of proven ability to increase market share, outperform competition, and maximize profits. Strategic planner: skilled at both short- and long-range goal setting. Easily establishes rapport and builds strong customer relations.

- ✓ Customer Focus
- ✓ Consistently Strong Sales Results
- ✓ Key Account Relationship Management
- ✓ Solution-Focused Account Service
- ✓ Territory Expansion
- ✓ New Product Introduction
- ✓ Pricing Strategies
- ✓ Profit Building and Growth

The beauty of this section is that it is also quite easy to customize. You simply need to plug in skills that are in the job posting (only if they're true for you, of course) and highlight the ones the potential employer is seeking. Remember *YOU* need to match the needs of the buyer—FIT is king in the job search!

A note about disclosing years of experience

One of the most frequently asked questions I get from candidates and clients over fifty is: "Should I list my years of experience?" The answer is "Yes and no," and "It's up to you." Now, how's that for being vague?

Nevertheless, it's true. You don't want to add anything to your resume that will eliminate you from getting through the door to the interview. As you well know, your resume is the marketing brochure for *YOU*. But, if you sell yourself as a far younger person, the truth will come out as soon as you meet face-to-face. That might lead the interviewer into feeling tricked—not a great way to make a first impression.

As you can see, our salesperson put "20 plus years" right at the top of her resume. And, at the beginning of this book, I wrote that my own experience as a career development and job search specialist was twenty years. In my personal and professional opinion, I think twenty years of experience is fine to state on one's resume. It shows that you, the applicant, have significant background and, therefore, highly developed skills in your field.

Yet I would not exceed the number "20." Beyond twenty years you're beginning to sound a bit long of tooth. You can, however, draw from our salesperson's profile and use the terms "20 plus years" or "over 20 years" if these suit your style. You are being honest and a bit vague at the same time. If you prefer not to disclose years at all, you can use terms like "significant experience" or "extensive experience."

The same 20-year caveat is true for your work history—your PROFESSIONAL EXPERIENCE section. Employers are mainly interested in the most recent ten to fifteen years of experience, so you don't need to go much beyond that. Nevertheless, if you want to show progression and earlier experience, you can show previous employment by simply listing company names and position titles without the years.

Now let's look at an abbreviated version of our salesperson's completed resume:

Terry Salesperson
2241 Jade Street
Tremont, New Jersey, O8601
terrysalesperson@.net

H (551) 555-3333 C (551) 555-2222

Sales Management Professional with 20 plus years of proven ability to increase market share, outperform competition, and maximize profits. Strategic planner: skilled at both short- and long-range goal setting. Easily establishes rapport and builds strong customer relations.

- ✓ Customer Focus
- ✓ Consistently Strong Sales Results
- ✓ Key Account Relationship Management
- ✓ Solution-Focused Account Service
- ✓ Territory Expansion
- ✓ New Product Introduction
- ✓ Pricing Strategies
- ✓ Profit Building and Growth

SELECTED ACCOMPLISHMENTS

- Achieved 40% increase in annual sales by spearheading and administering strategic marketing and advertising campaign.
- Accomplished double-digit sales within first year in new accounts position and expanded territory to $6 million plus in annual sales.
- Recognized for four consecutive years as "Salesperson of the Year" at XYZ Company, outperforming 200 other vendors.

PROFESSIONAL EXPERIENCE

GET IT CHEAP, Tremont, New Jersey 2003 – Present
Account Manager/Sales Representative

- Exceeded annual sales objectives by 25% due to sound sales acumen and active prospecting.
- Cultivated business relationships with over 250 new clients in the United States, Mexico, and Canada, within a 12-month period.
- Launched product promotions, establishing successful business relations in printing publishing, and media markets.
- Increased customer retention levels by 15% within highly competitive markets by providing excellent customer service.

HOTSHOT SALES, Austin, Texas 1998 – 2003
Sales Representative

- Ranked as one of the company's top five account managers by consistently exceeding monthly and annual goals.
- Increased product line sales by 20% through conducting end-user calls and consumer seminars.
- Provided total customer satisfaction by professionally responding to needs of over 300 accounts: ensured order accuracy and identified future needs.

PREVIOUS EXPERIENCE

BUY IT NOW, Dallas, Texas, *Sales Representative*
SO GOOD FOR YOU, Dallas, Texas, *Sales Trainee*

ONGOING PROFESSIONAL DEVELOPMENT

Seminar presentation training

Sales training for consumer products

Professional selling skills courses

MS Office (Word, Excel and PowerPoint)

Additional Notes

"References Available Upon Request" does not appear on the salesperson's resume. This fact is assumed and the phrase is also considered passé, so don't use it. Additionally, there is no "Hobbies" section. A resume is a written document of your *professional* skills and experience. You may wish to include board memberships or memberships in professional organizations. Other than these, I do not suggest listing additional affiliations unless they have a direct bearing on your career. Avoid fancy stuff like the use of color in headings. Tried and true, black ink on white or cream cotton bond paper is best.

New career direction resume

But what if you're looking to do something else? How can you create a resume to highlight your skills and experience, yet focus them toward a different career?

To do this, you'll need to stress your transferable skills (remember these are skills that transfer from one arena to another). You do, however, have a choice as far as formatting and can go in a couple of different directions. You can create a functional resume wherein you list your skills and experience under skill headings. You'll put these at the top of your resume and add your job titles at the bottom. (Go to the Internet to find examples of a functional resume.) But most resume reviewers are not in favor of functional resumes because they think you're trying to hide something in your work experience or mislead them in some way.

Therefore, you might consider using the combination format in this case as well. Let's see how our salesperson turned her resume into supporting a new career as a marketing communications specialist. Remember, whatever you put on your resume must be 100 percent truthful, but it is your choice as to how you wish to emphasize your experience. In the salesperson's case, about 30 percent of her work experience dealt with public relations and creating marketing materials. So, because she wants to shift her career to the communications side, she will place her emphasis on Marketing/Communications.

Also, if you're shifting career focus, it behooves you to get some training in that area before doing a lot of active job seeking. You'll want to add as much as possible to your credentials to show you can handle the job—so don't forget to note any classes or certifications on your resume. Although education and training usually go at the end of a resume, in this case, you'll cite the training at the top as well.

Time to hit the books and build new skills!

Here's the top part of Terry Salesperson's resume focusing on her new career direction:

Terry Salesperson
2241 Jade Street
Tremont, New Jersey, O8601
terrysalesperson@.net

H (551) 555-3333 C (551) 555-2222

Marketing Communications Specialist with 20 plus years' demonstrated skill in creating eye-catching and effective marketing materials. Media savvy with expertise in:

- ✓ Public Relations
- ✓ Web Site Management
- ✓ Media Relations
- ✓ Print Production
- ✓ Press Releases
- ✓ New Product Introduction
- ✓ Pricing Strategies
- ✓ Trade Shows

SELECTED ACCOMPLISHMENTS

- Achieved 40% increase in annual sales by spearheading and administering strategic marketing and advertising campaign.
- Expanded customer base by 200% within a 12-month period by building an active web presence, developing strong marketing materials, and aggressively promoting new product launch.
- Consistently streamlined sales efforts by developing, leading, and executing regular communication strategy meetings.
- Successfully completed a 9-month "Advanced Marketing Strategies" class as well as 6 one-day seminars on building client base through proven client relationship techniques.

PROFESSIONAL EXPERIENCE

GET IT CHEAP, Tremont, New Jersey 2007 – Present
Marketing and Sales Representative

- Exceeded annual sales objectives by 25% due to active marketing promotions and sound sales acumen.
- Cultivated business relationships with over 250 new clients in the United States, Mexico, and Canada, within a 12-month period through effective outreach and public relations techniques.
- Launched product promotions, establishing successful business relations in printing, publishing, and media markets.
- Increased customer retention levels within highly competitive markets by implementing excellent client relationship management practices.

Now it's your turn!
You now have the tools and expertise to create a product brochure (your resume) for *YOU*. And, if you follow the suggestions for highlighting your skill sets, creating your winning examples, and focusing on results by placing them to the left of your bulleted statements, your resume will "knock their socks off!"

For additional ideas simply go to the Internet—there are loads of examples. Just type, "sample resumes" into your favorite search engine. A site to get you started is: http://www.bestsampleresume.com. To find specific careers, type "sample resumes for sales," "sample resumes for administrative assistant," and so forth. However, beware! Even many of the so-called "experts" put dates to the left or use blocks of text (paragraphs) to describe work experience. But you know better! By using these proven and effective techniques, you'll make a dynamite first impression and maximize your chances for opening the door to the job of your dreams!

Put the pieces together and create a resume that rocks!

STRATEGY FOUR: ACTION STEPS

Before you start ~

Step back a moment before your begin your resume or revise your existing one. As this will be your product brochure, you want to make certain it is advertising you in a way that will serve your ultimate goals:

- Be sure your motivated skills are well represented.
- Do *NOT* highlight skills you dislike using. If you place these types of skills prominently on your resume, you can be certain employers will hire you with the expectation you'll be performing them.
- Review your ten winning example statements from Strategy Two, determine the skill sets they hold in common, and what these similarities suggest for you to find work you will love. Play to your strengths and activities you enjoy—remember your resume is a *future-oriented* document!

Add these types of phrases to strengthen your professional profile:

- Skilled and effective in...
- Demonstrated ability to...
- Proven skills in...
- Professional reputation as...
- Collaborated effectively to...
- Have a unique combination of...
- Proven track record of...
- Resourceful problem solver with...

Use descriptive words to highlight your results:

Achieved
Augmented
Broadened
Developed
Doubled
Drove
Effected
Eliminated
Empowered
Exceeded
Expanded
Improved
Increased
Maximized
Minimized
Multiplied
Produced
Reduced
Saved
Tripled
Turned Around

Action Verbs

Here are sample action verbs listed under skill categories. Recall the skill areas you identified in Strategy One as ones you particularly enjoy, and make certain your resume reflects these motivated skills.

Helping	Creative	Detail	Management	Analytical	Physical
assisted	conceptualized	arranged	administered	diagnosed	assembled
coached	customized	cataloged	assigned	evaluated	built
counseled	designed	classified	chaired	examined	devised
educated	developed	compiled	coordinated	identified	engineered
guided	fashioned	executed	delegated	inspected	fabricated
motivated	illustrated	filed	executed	investigated	moved
referred	performed	implemented	oversaw	organized	operated
supported	revised	monitored	planned	surveyed	remodeled
taught	shaped	recorded	prioritized	systemized	repaired
trained	strategized	systematized	supervised	theorized	sorted

Resume Worksheet

Name: ____

Address: ____
(consider removing if posting online)

City, State, Zip ______________________________________

Phone: ____________________ home ____________________ cell

E-mail: ___________________________________

Fax: ____________________________________
(optional)

Professional profile:

Desired position (in bold) _______________________ with

Experience level: ____

Demonstrated skills in: ____________________________________

____

____

Skills table (easily customized to position requirements)

SELECTED ACCOMPLISHMENTS
(results highlighted to the left)

- ____
- ____
- ____
- ____
- ____

PROFESSIONAL EXPERIENCE

____

Company (all caps), City, State Years of Employment

____

Position title (italicized)

Responsibility statement (optional):

____

____

____

Winning example statements with results highlighted to the left whenever possible:

- ____
- ____
- ____
- ____
- ____
- ____

____

Company (all caps), City, State Years of Employment

____

Position title (italicized)

Responsibility statement (optional):

____

____

____

Winning example statements with results highlighted to the left whenever possible:

- ____
- ____
- ____
- ____
- ____
- ____

____

Company (all caps), City, State Years of Employment

____

Position title (italicized)

Responsibility statement (optional):

____

____

____

Winning example statements with results highlighted to the left whenever possible:

- ____
- ____
- ____
- ____
- ____
- ____

____

Company (all caps), City, State Years of Employment

____

Position title (italicized)

Responsibility statement (optional):

____

____

____

Winning example statements with results highlighted to the left whenever possible:

- ____
- ____
- ____
- ____
- ____
- ____

EDUCATION

____

Degree School City, State

ONGOING PROFESSIONAL DEVELOPMENT

____

____

____

____

Next up: a catchy commercial all about YOU!

STRATEGY FIVE: CREATE YOUR CATCHY COMMERCIAL (AKA YOUR BRANDING STATEMENT)

Your branding statement is a way to introduce yourself so you capture the listener's interest, make yourself memorable, and distinguish yourself from the competition. The technique has gone by several names including "elevator speech" and "30-second commercial" because it's a brief statement about who you are and the skills you have to offer. In this world of information overload, you'll need to get your message across quickly, clearly, and succinctly.

We've all heard of the importance of branding and making products and services stand out from the competition. As a critical component to any branding effort, it is essential you spend some time creating a brief statement that defines *YOU*: your unique strengths, qualities, experience level, and areas of expertise.

Briefly stating your background appears deceptively easy—a "no brainer." I invite you to give it a try. Close your eyes and imagine you are asked to describe your business experience and your areas of expertise in a few sentences using about half a minute's time. My guess is, if you haven't previously rehearsed this technique, you'll find it rather difficult. This simple statement requires time and thought. However, it represents one of your most essential and critical marketing tools: a clear and memorable statement that plays to your strengths and sets you apart from the competition.

My personal experience

I found the branding statement to be extremely helpful in building my private practice as a career counselor and job search specialist. Years ago, when I didn't know how to present myself, I'd respond to "What do you do?" with "I'm a career counselor." This was often a conversation stopper; people just moved on to something else and changed the subject.

After learning the critical elements and designing my own catchy commercial, this changed. From then on I was able to engage my listeners far more effectively. Our conversation often produced leads or business opportunities when they said, "I know someone who needs to meet with you."

Here is an example of how I might introduce myself now

"I've been a career transition counselor and job search specialist for twenty years and I work with people who are unhappy with their career direction. I help them regain their enthusiasm for work by showing them how to identify their special talents and skills, uncover where their passions lie, and discover their dream job. Then I make sure they land it by teaching them the job search strategies that produce real results. I'm thrilled to say my clients tell me our work together has truly changed their lives for the better and that's my goal—helping people find work where they'll thrive and grow is as good as it gets. They're happy and fulfilled and I am, too!"

As you design your branding statement, once again, it's helpful to think of yourself as a product competing with other products. You'll need to convey your level of experience, your skill sets relevant to the needs of your audience, any appropriate personal strengths or traits, and the benefits you can and will provide. Remember that potential employers have needs or problems they are trying to solve. When you present yourself as a competent professional who can address and resolve these issues, you're setting yourself up as the answer to their prayers.

Your catchy commercial consists of the following components—

Your level and type of experience:

- How long have you been doing what you do?
- In which environments have you gained your experience? Do you have a corporate background; have you worked in private practice; are you familiar with the needs of start-up organizations? Have you acquired your skills in a variety of environments?

Your top skill sets:

- What are your special strengths and areas of expertise?
- How can you distinguish yourself from the competition?
- How are your skills relevant to the needs of today's marketplace and potential employers?

Relevant personal traits:

- Are you detail-oriented; do you see the big picture; are you able to think outside the box?
- Are you especially adept at building alliances, a team player, and a consensus builder?
- Do you thrive while working under pressure; do you have an ability to handle several tasks simultaneously?

Benefits you can provide:

- Why would an employer want to talk with you?
- Which results have you produced in the past you consider as being especially memorable?
- What is your added value?

How might this person help you?
(This is used in networking situations.)

- Can this person supply you with names and introductions?
- Are you needing information and advice?
- What can they tell you about companies/positions you're targeting?

In addition, to be truly effective, your branding statement must adapt to your audience. You need to have the basics of your introduction so well practiced that you can adjust them on the spot to match the focus of the person with whom you are speaking. You have to come across saying the right things at the right level. A catchy commercial that might be great for the Chamber of

Commerce mixer might not work so well when introducing yourself at the church social. You'll want to be sure to spread the word whenever you can, so make certain you know it well enough to cover your points *and* adjust it to your audience.

Time to be your own torchbearer!

Let's take a look at our salesperson's catchy commercial

"I've been in sales for over twenty years and I've been told I can sell ice to an Eskimo. Actually, I'm proud to say I've got a track record that includes creating a campaign that increased sales by 40 percent for one organization and brought in over 250 new clients for another—both within a year's time. I'm looking for a start-up company that's expanding quickly and needs someone with proven sales skills to increase their customer base and close the deal. Do you have any suggestions of companies I might research, or people I might speak with who'd be able to give me some ideas and contacts?"

Now it's your turn!
Remember—you'll want to grab your listeners' interest, make it memorable, get your skills and experience across, and set yourself apart. This can be one of the most difficult pieces of marketing *YOU* because, again, most of us don't care to sell ourselves. But take a deep breath and get going: it *has* to be done!

Here are a few tips to make things a bit easier:

- Use speech softeners. Rather than saying, "I'm great at this," "I'm superb at that," etc., you can use phrases such as "I've been told," "people say," "I like to think that," "I pride myself on," and so forth.
- You've already written most of your branding statement if you've written your resume. It's at the beginning of your Professional Profile section. Actually, for consistency's sake, you'll want the two to be very similar.
- Both your product brochure and your catchy commercial are ways to brand *YOU* and make you stand apart from the competition. Just like those of us over fifty know exactly what *It Takes a Lickin' and Keeps on Tickin'* refers to; you'll want to brand yourself in a way that makes you memorable and unique.

Your branding statement will require practice and constant revision. It's usually helpful to write your thoughts down and then practice them out loud. However, writing that appears articulate and well stated on paper, can seem stilted and inappropriate when spoken. So be sure to modify your thoughts and words as you practice aloud.

Although it may seem tedious, this particular exercise is well worth the effort. This simple technique will guide you to express yourself, your skill set, and your background with clarity and confidence. Develop your own catchy commercial and see how it gives you that all-important winning first impression.

Your 10-second attention grabber

Another version of the catchy commercial is brief (a mere 10-seconds or so), but it packs a wallop! It's used in very informal settings: a backyard barbecue, neighborhood get together, swim party, or the like. Say something a bit quirky or off the wall when asked what you do. This will draw the attention of your listeners and they'll immediately want to know more.

For example, I might say, "I help people on the feisty side of fifty land the job they love." One of my workshop participants was a buyer and she used the line, "I shop with other people's money." But my all time favorite was a man who'd played a role in developing satellite radio. He smiled and answered, "I work with the lunatic fringe of show business!"

So come up with a 10-second grabber of your own and have fun with it. You'll definitely make people want to ask you more about what you do. Then you can move into your more serious branding statement and give them an idea of the type of work you're looking for.

Remember what you learned in scouts

Be sure to plan ahead and *be prepared!* Whether you find yourself in formal networking situations or in line at the grocery story, you'll want to be prepared with a memorable statement that describes your strengths and experience. You never know who might be your next connection to a job you will love!

STRATEGY FIVE: ACTION STEPS

Create your branding statement ~

____

____

____

____

____

____

____

____

____

____

____

Write out your 10-second attention grabber ~

____

____

____

Now that we've got your product brochure and your catchy commercial in place, let's move on to your product launch...

STRATEGY SIX: GET THE WORD OUT

Anyone over fifty has heard this saying a thousand times: "It's not *what* you know, it's *who* you know." And, just because it's a wee bit on the stale side, doesn't make the meaning of it any the less true—especially when it relates to landing a job you'll love. Networking is, by far, the most effective way to get yourself in front of key decision makers and hiring managers.

Uh oh! I can hear your teeth grinding right now. First I ask you to highlight your accomplishments on paper; then I push you into creating a verbal commercial touting your abilities, and now this? For people who hate to sell themselves, isn't this taking things way too far? Well—actually, *NO!*

Time to take another deep breath because I'm going to give you the reasons you not only have to network, you have to network consistently and well.

Most jobs are obtained through networking

Despite the wealth of Internet job sites, studies show that somewhat more than 75 percent of positions are obtained through personal referral. The percentage is even greater for older workers and those in higher-level positions. Let's take a look at why this is true...

Your competition levels can drop dramatically

Suppose our salesperson friend decided to respond to an online posting for a senior sales position. She's one out of 1,500 to apply—not uncommon in today's market. However, our salesperson knew her background was well suited to the position and took the trouble to customize her resume. Because she did this, her resume was one of the 100 resumes that were flagged by the scanning software to be viewed by a human resources representative.

But the HR rep was told to submit only the top twenty resumes to the hiring manager. Luckily for our salesperson, her resume just happened to land toward the top of the stack of resumes the rep reviewed—and he liked what he saw. In fact, once the HR rep found twenty suitable ones, he threw the rest out. "Why waste any more of my time?" was his thought as he dropped the twenty chosen resumes on the hiring manager's desk.

The hiring manager made a cursory review of the resumes before her and selected her top twelve for a phone screen interview. These went back to HR and the rep contacted each of the applicants and asked a set of basic questions to ascertain that they actually had the requisite skills and experience for the position. He also asked them about their salary requirements hoping to weed out those who wanted too much (overqualified or too greedy) or too little (uncertain about their qualifications or desperate).

Finally the stack was whittled down to the seven who were called in for a face-to-face interview. Our salesperson was overjoyed to be among those selected to come in. After a long day of interviews (five in all), she was asked to return for another round. Now, she was even more excited because she really wanted the job and seemed to be heading towards an offer. After the second day, she was told that she was one of three under final consideration.

Unfortunately our salesperson was not selected. The other two candidates each had personal referrals from within the company and one had a recommendation from several customers as well.

Our friend, the salesperson, just couldn't compete with that. And, adding to her distress, she later found out the candidate who did land the job (the one who had the customers' blessings) hadn't even submitted a resume through the online posting. Although he'd gone through the proper HR channels, his resume was hand-walked in by his friend and placed on the desk of the hiring manager.

The salesperson sighed: *"It's not what you know it's who you know!"*

Let's briefly recap

Without networking*:* The salesperson's initial competition level was one out of 1,500.

With networking: The winning applicant's initial competition level was one out of twelve. At a minimum, personal referrals from trusted employees will usually generate a phone screen interview.

With networking: The winning applicant's competition level was more likely one out of two. Because the top candidates each had similar backgrounds and skill levels, the personal referrals were the deciding factor.

Other reasons to network

You'll meet new people with fresh ideas and contacts.
By attending events where you'll run into a number of people, you'll expand your circle of friends and contacts exponentially. Armed with a strong and confident branding statement, you'll be setting the stage to gather lots of helpful names and information.

Remember networking is a two-way street. You'll want to create mutually beneficial relationships where you share ideas and resources. Plan on keeping in touch by e-mail and through phone calls and, whenever you can, pass along any pieces of helpful information.

You'll break through to the hidden job market.
Some career experts believe that as many as 80 percent of new positions go unadvertised. Employers want to avoid the time and expense involved in reviewing a flood of incoming resumes so they're turning more toward employee networks and personal referrals.

This is even more valid for smaller companies, where most jobs are to be found. It is also truer when openings are scarce. Employers want to know as much as possible about new hires to eliminate bringing in any dreaded bad apples who might spoil their team. Equally, if not more important than work-specific skills, personal traits such as integrity, a willingness to cooperate, and a strong work ethic are prized. These kinds of strengths are assumed if a recommendation comes from a valued employee.

Some positions are in the process of being created and haven't yet made it out of the planning stages. If your networking partner submits your name early on, this can greatly cut down on any potential competition for the job.

There are a hundred other reasons why networking is key to landing a job you will love. Hopefully I've convinced you of its importance. Better yet, this is another area where people over fifty have a decided advantage. We have a lifetime of relationships built up over the years including family, friends, coworkers, customers, clients, fellow club and church members, professionals we've hired (e.g., doctors, lawyers, CPAs), to name a few. Also, our business connections are generally with people our own age. So many of those in our network will be in senior positions and will have connections with key decision makers.

Whenever possible, network in person

A friendly face makes for a far more immediate and stronger contact than a voice over the phone and, most definitely, more than an e-mail.

Tell everyone and anyone

Okay, your Aunt Tillie probably doesn't know the CEO of the software company where you'd like to work. But you have no way of knowing that the CEO is the father of the boy who cuts her lawn unless you talk with her about your job search goals. In other words, do not eliminate people just because you don't see a clear connection to your targeted position.

Make a list of at least twenty names to start your networking and plan to make contact. You'll especially want to network with those who work with a lot of people: accountants, travel agents, and insurance agents are a few suggestions. My personal favorite is my hair stylist. Whenever I hear of a job opening, I tell her. She knows *everyone!*

Be sure to use your catchy commercial

This is the main reason you'll want to know your branding statement so well that you can easily adjust it to your audience. It's critical your friends and contacts know what you're looking for.

Many clients have told me, as soon as their friends heard they were laid off, they started giving out their names to people they knew. They also recommended them for job openings—many times without asking. Although the well-meaning friends meant to be helpful, these proved embarrassing situations because the "helpful" friends had only a limited idea of what my clients were looking to do. You can avoid these types of sticky situations and get the referrals you want by giving each and every one of your contacts a rendition of your catchy commercial and supplying them with a copy of your resume.

Go beyond your immediate circle

Most jobs are gotten through personal referrals but these referrals do not usually come from close friends. Rather, positions are obtained through "friends of friends of friends." In other words, there are several linked connections between the jobseeker and the referral source. (Think: *Six Degrees of Separation!*) That is why two of the most effective questions you can ask are: "Do you know anyone who might be able to give me some additional information on ABC Company?" or "Do you have any additional contacts at XYZ Corporation who might be willing to talk with me?"

Target your search and network your way into companies

One of the most effective ways of landing a job you'll love is to target companies or businesses where you'd like to work and then network your way through the door by contacting people on the inside. Here's how you do it:

Start by reviewing your research:

- How might your own career path fit within the overall organizational structure?
- How would your skills, knowledge, and experience best serve this employer?
- How large is the company and what are the hiring needs?

- How profitable is the firm and what is the financial outlook for the future?
- What are the values, mission statement, and general culture of the organization?
- What are the recent developments in the field that might impact the company?
- Are there any changes in upper management, location, or competitors that could affect your chances of being hired?
- Additional facts you should know...

Armed with this knowledge, you'll customize your product brochure (resume) and your catchy commercial. Then pull out your list of the networking contacts you know personally and either phone or e-mail them. Whichever method you choose, let them know you are targeting XYZ Company. Ask them if they know anyone who works there, or even if they know anyone who might know someone who works there. If they come up with a referral, ask them if you can contact that person and use their name.

Making a "down-the-line" contact
You now have a name and contact information so you'll want to follow this process—

E-mail your contact requesting a meeting
Here's an example of how to do it:

> "John Doe *(your mutual contact)* suggested I get in touch with you because, with your extensive knowledge and proven ability in widget sales *(a tiny schmooze here)*, you might be willing to give me some advice.
>
> I have twenty years in product sales and pride myself on a track record that includes creating a campaign that increased sales by 40% for one organization and bringing in over 250 new clients for another—both within a year's time *(a version of your branding statement).*

I would very much appreciate any suggestions you might have for me and will be contacting you early next week to see if we might set up a 15-minute appointment. *(Ask for a brief appointment with a specific time limit. Everyone is busy so, if you just request a meeting, they will more than likely decline. If, however, you put your mutual contact's name at the top of your e-mail and then add a request for either 15 or 20 minutes, people are much more likely to accept.)*

Thank you in advance for your time."

Follow up at the promised time with a phone call

"My name is Sally Supergirl and I e-mailed you last week. John Doe suggested I get in touch..." *(repeat the basic script of your e-mail).*

End with: "I'd like to see if we might arrange a brief meeting at a time and place that's convenient for you. It won't take longer than 15 minutes and I'd appreciate any advice you'd be willing to give me."

The networking meeting

When you're conducting your face-to-face meeting, be certain you don't give the impression you're asking for a job. If you do, the person with whom you're networking could feel like they've been deceived. Your visit is for information gathering *only* and a chance to learn from his or her experience, knowledge of the company, and, most of all, to make another ally in your job search.

- Dress like this is a regular job interview—you are making a first impression with someone inside your targeted company and you want to look your best.
- Be on time and come prepared with a list of questions.
- Ask if you can take notes and, if so, take them. Writing down information shows that you're interested and that you care enough to want to remember the suggestions they're giving you.

It's best to ask your questions in a certain order. Here are some sample questions you may wish to use:

1. Ask questions about the person. People generally like to talk about themselves so you will engage them in the interview right away.

    - What is a typical day like for you around here?
    - How did you break into this field?
    - What do you most enjoy about your job?
    - What excites you about this business?

2. Ask advice questions:

    - Would you mind briefly reviewing my resume and giving me any suggestions that might make it stronger?
    - Do you think I need additional training to be more competitive?
    - Which parts of my background do you think would be the best fit for this organization?
    - Which types of individuals thrive in the company culture and succeed around here?

3. At the end of your meeting, ask for additional referrals:

    - You've been so helpful. Do you know anyone else who might be willing to give me his or her perspective on the field/organization? I won't ask for more than 15 minutes of their time—and may I use your name?

A couple of days after the networking meeting, send a thank you e-mail or note expressing your gratitude for their advice and listing specific ways you have or will follow up on their suggestions:

- "Thank you for suggesting I contact Mary Marketer. We have an appointment set up for next week."
- "Thank you for suggesting I read the article in *Salesperson*

Weekly. I've done so and found it to be extremely helpful."

- End your networking message with "Thanks again and I will keep you apprised of my progress." That way, you've opened the door to contacting them from time to time.

This is networking at it's finest. You are meeting face-to-face with people within your targeted company, making a great first impression, and your contacts are growing. When something comes up in the hidden job market that would suit you, you are very likely to find yourself at the top of their list.

Send them your resume

You do not necessarily want to leave your resume with your contact at the first meeting. Again, you don't want to appear as if you're asking for a job. Your meeting was for informational purposes only. However, they may very well ask for your resume and, in that case, you'll certainly want to give it to them.

Nevertheless, your follow-up thank you is the perfect time to include your resume or attach it to an e-mail. You might add the phrase: "I'm enclosing (attaching) my resume for your information" or "I've followed the suggestions you gave me regarding my resume and wanted you to see the updated version."

Business cards

You do want to leave anyone with whom you've had a networking encounter with your business card. This is an easy and convenient way to provide them with your contact information. But do not leave it at that! Your business card should list your job title (just because you may be currently unemployed does not mean you've lost your title) and several key skills you can provide.

Here's our salesperson's business card:

Terry Salesperson
Sales Management Professional
Tremont, New Jersey, 08601
terrysalesperson@.net
H (551) 555-3333 • C (551) 555-2222

Customer Focus	Territory Expansion
Consistently Strong Sales	New Product Introduction

Notice that she left off the street address but retained the city and state information. Most people want to know where you're located. However, for the sake of privacy, you may choose to eliminate your address. You can leave your address off your resume as well, and I would suggest doing so if you're posting your resume online. In that case, you'll likely want to disclose your zip code and cell phone information only.

A word about e-mail

Since you'll be doing a lot of networking and responding to online postings, it's a good idea to open a separate e-mail account solely for your job search. That way, anything that's directed at your search is easy to locate and won't clog your general inbox.

Use social networking sites

Although I'm still a proponent of actual face-to-face meetings, social networking sites like LinkedIn can prove invaluable tools to making contacts within your targeted organizations. After you've identified your companies of interest, you can link your way into the organization and set up informational meetings with people inside the firm.

Go to the upper right hand corner of your LinkedIn page and enter the name of one of your target companies in the search tool provided. There's a good chance it will be listed because LinkedIn has become a commonly used networking tool for applicants, employees, and businesses. You'll find an overview of the firm and any links you may have with current and former personnel. Pay special attention to recent changes in management. As we mentioned in Strategy Three, both new hires and recently departed employees are signals that there may be openings and real opportunities for you.

Also, there's a "Jobs" section at the top of your LinkedIn page. If you click on it, the site will display job openings that will likely align with your own job search goals. This is because LinkedIn identifies these openings through the keywords you've chosen to include in your profile. Then, after you select listings that appeal to you, follow the procedure you use with your personal contacts and network your way into the organization.

Additionally, many companies are using recommendations on LinkedIn as ways to prescreen candidates and, often, even in lieu of more traditional references. Be certain to ask managers, department heads, co-workers, clients, and customers to recommend you. This can go a long way to securing an interview.

You'll also want to make sure your LinkedIn profile is current and that it substantiates how you're describing yourself on your resume and in your cover letter. Although you'll be customizing both resumes and cover letters, the information should basically be the same as that in your online profile. Since you're highlighting your professional experience and gathering a list of impressive recommendations, it's also a good idea to add a hyperlink to your LinkedIn profile on your job search correspondence.

Both Facebook and Twitter can also prove valuable online tools for jobseekers. Facebook and SimplyHired.com have combined resources to alert you to openings at companies where your Facebook friends work. So, once you've spotted a position you feel would be a good fit, you can contact your friends and take it from there.

Twitter has a find feature that works for both individuals and companies. After entering the name of a company that interests you, you can choose to follow key employees (such as the Director of Human Resources) within the organization and begin a Twitter dialogue. This is another way to connect with people who may prove helpful to your search.

One important caveat: However you choose to present yourself online, know that the information is likely to become a permanent part of the Internet. It will be available to whoever might be searching under your name. Make sure you are presenting yourself professionally and in good taste at all times. Often we think of Facebook and Twitter as being social networking sites where we share personal information such as family photos and the like. That's all well and good—but recruiters and Human Resources professionals may also view what you post. Most companies are now requiring that their hiring staff conduct online research on candidates, and over half of the reps confess to rejecting applicants based upon questionable information they found online. They can and will eliminate you from their pool of applicants if they don't like what they see!

Another method of approach

As you're doing research online or through the print media, you may come across news articles that mention key players within your target organizations. If you can uncover their contact information, you might send them an introductory e-mail/letter something like this: "I've read the recent article in *XYZ News* about your innovative approach to marketing interactive games to older adults. As a marketing manager with a background in software sales, I admire the pioneering work you've done at Gaming for Seniors, Inc. I'd love the opportunity to discuss your ideas further, and would like to set up a brief meeting at your convenience. I recognize you're busy so it won't take longer than 15 minutes."

So there you have it! Since networking is the most effective means to landing a job (recall at least 75 percent of positions are found through networking) that means you'll want to spend about 75 percent of your job search time doing it. Networking has the added benefit of reducing the feeling of isolation some jobseekers experience. You'll be out and about meeting new people, contacting old friends, and spreading the word. If you write down and monitor your networking contacts (and I highly recommend that you do), you'll also have a way of tangibly tracking your progress. Even though it may take a while to start getting actual job interviews, by jotting down notes such as "made 7 calls" and "wrote 15 e-mails," you'll realize that you are moving forward toward your end result: finding and landing the job you will love!

Spread the word about YOU the product!

STRATEGY SIX: ACTION STEPS

Make a list of contacts and the information you want (referrals, company information, general job search information, etc.) Don't forget to list people who work with the public, e.g., accountants, lawyers, salesmen, etc.

Name: Desired information:

Name: Desired information:

____

____

____

____

____

____

____

____

____

____

____

____

____

Now it's time to learn how to write the two most important letters of your job search…

STRATEGY SEVEN: THE POWER OF THE WRITTEN WORD

You'll want any correspondence you send out to reflect both your abilities and your professionalism. In addition to networking e-mails and notes, there are a couple of standard forms of written communication that can make or break your chances for success. We will focus on the two main ones: the cover letter and the interview thank you note.

The cover letter
Although, at times, only a resume is required, there are numerous instances when you'll need to create an effective cover letter. The purpose of the cover letter is to grab the attention of the reader and garner their interest in reading your resume.

Many clients have told me they struggled for hours composing a two-page cover letter explaining why they are the perfect person for the job. This is totally unnecessary! Cover letters need to be effective, but they are relatively easy and straightforward to write.

You'll follow many of the same guidelines you used with your resume:

- Make it brief (no one wants to wade through a two-page cover letter*)*.
- Make it eye friendly (use bullets and white space when describing your skills and accomplishments in paragraph two). You'll want to make certain the information is readily accessible to the reader.
- Customize (just like with your resume): prepare a template cover letter and adjust it to meet the requirements of the advertised posting or ad.

There are basically three paragraphs in a cover letter:

- Paragraph one—Name the position you are applying for; display some knowledge of the company with an added bit of schmooze.
- Paragraph two—Display your strengths and experience: why they would want to read your resume and call you in for an interview. (Basically your branding statement.)
- Paragraph three—Suggest an interview and display your enthusiasm for the position. You will want your contact information readily available; even if it's already on your heading, you may wish to list it at the end of your letter as well.

Example of our salesperson's cover letter:

Terry Salesperson
2241 Jade Street
Tremont, New Jersey, O8601
terrysalesperson@.net

H (551) 555-3333 C (551) 555-2222

Dear Human Resources Representative:

(*It's always best to use a name if you can find one. However, "Dear Human Resources Representative" and "Dear Hiring Manager" are also okay. Do not use the tired and trite "To Whom It May Concern."*)

I am responding to your February 2nd advertisement for a Senior Sales Representative. I'm especially interested in finding out more about the position because I've been tracking your company for years and am well aware of its fine reputation in the financial services field.

(A tiny schmooze that let's them know you've done your research and know about their company and its reputation.)

I have twenty years of varied sales experience, the past ten being in the financial services industry, and bring the following skills and accomplishments:

- Consistently strong sales: Achieved double-digit sales within my first year in new accounts.
- Territory expansion: Expanded territory to $4 million plus in annual sales within a twelve-month period.
- Customer focus and service: Recognized for four consecutive years as "Salesperson of the Year" by XYZ Company.

(Bullet this paragraph. Bullets will make your strengths and accomplishments eye friendly and literally "leap off the page.")

I am very interested in discussing this most exciting opportunity further and can be reached by e-mail, or by phone at either (551) 555-3333 (home) or (551) 555-2222 (cell). I look forward to hearing from you soon.

Sincerely,

Terry Salesperson

The interview thank you note/e-mail

The second main type of written communication is a critical piece of follow-up you'll *need* to do. You'd be surprised at the number of applicants who don't follow up after an interview. So, by sending a thank you note, you've already distinguished yourself and landed on the interviewer's desk with another positive impression.

As with cover letters there are a few general guidelines:

- Make it brief (no need to go on and on, they've already met with you).
- If you've done a series of interviews or a group interview, be sure and ask everyone for a business card so you will have their contact information. You'll want to write a short thank you to each of them.

- There are differences of opinion as to sending a handwritten note, a typed note, or an e-mail. Many feel that a handwritten thank you shows more effort and thoughtfulness than something typed or e-mailed. If, however, you're going for a position in a field that prizes high tech, you are always better served by an e-mail. Also, if your handwriting is difficult to read, this would be another reason to either type or e-mail your thank you.
- Another area of contention is how quickly your thank you note should land on the interviewer's desk. Some job search experts say the next day is ideal. Nevertheless, this is not always the case. If you were one of the very first candidates to be interviewed, some of your strengths may be forgotten as they speak with additional candidates. By sending a well-written thank you that arrives several days after the interview, you'll be reminding them of your good manners, your strengths, and your professionalism.

There are also three basic paragraphs in a thank you note:

- Paragraph one—Genuinely thank your interviewer for his or her time.
- Paragraph two—Sell yourself once again by reemphasizing how your skills and experience match with the position requirements. (Do not use bullets this time.)
- Paragraph three—Be certain to reconfirm your interest and enthusiasm in the position and the company.

Here's another example from our friend, the salesperson:

Terry Salesperson
2241 Jade Street
Tremont, New Jersey, O8601
terrysalesperson@.net

H (551) 555-3333 C (551) 555-2222

Dear Mr. Smith,

Thank you very much for the opportunity to meet with you last Tuesday to discuss the Senior Sales position. I appreciate the time you spent giving me additional details on both the company and the job.

(Show your appreciation for the time and information the interviewer gave you.)

I feel certain that my background in financial services' sales will prove a valuable asset to your organization and I would be excited to bring my strong customer service, marketing, and territory expansion skills to the work you described.

(Soft sell yourself to the position and reconfirm that you are a perfect fit for what they're looking for.)

After our conversation, I'm even more enthusiastic about the position and your organization. I look forward to hearing from you at your earliest convenience.

(Express that enthusiasm once again!)

Sincerely,

Note: As with resumes, there are loads of sample job search letters on the Internet. Enter either "sample cover letters" or "interview thank you letter examples" into your search engine and check them out for phrases and wording you like. Just be sure to remember the basic guidelines. There are a number of sample letters on the Internet that are either too wordy or otherwise inappropriate, so stick with what you know will get you results!

STRATEGY SEVEN: ACTION STEPS

Create a template cover letter ~

Your Contact Information

Date:

Dear Human Resources Representative:

I am responding to your advertisement for________________________________

____

I'm especially interested in finding out more about the position because I am well aware of your organization's fine reputation as a _______________________

____

____

I have X years of experience in the XYZ field and bring the following skills and accomplishments:

- ____
- ____
- ____
- ____

I'm very interested in discussing this exciting opportunity further and can be reached at...

Sincerely,

Create a template thank you letter ~

Your Contact Information

Date:

Dear Mr. Jones:

Thank you very much for the opportunity to meet with you on __________(date) to discuss the ________________ position. I appreciate the time you spent giving me additional details on both the company and the job.

I feel certain that my background in… (*sell yourself again by emphasizing your skill set and fit with the position requirements*).

____

____

____

____

____

After our conversation, I'm even more enthusiastic about the position and your organization. I look forward to hearing from you at your earliest convenience.

Sincerely,

Now it's on to your big moment—It's Showtime!

STRATEGY EIGHT: KNOCK 'EM DEAD INTERVIEWS!

This is it! You've been called in for the all-important interview with the hiring manager and you want to do your best. Like many other aspects in life, the key to success is preparation. We will cover how to get ready for this significant event in great detail. However, as many of you reading this may not have been on an interview in years, let's start by going over the basics.

The Interviewer has several goals on his/her agenda:

- Do you have the skills and experience to do the job?
- Can you speak to the examples on your resume and explain them in detail?
- Are you willing to do what it takes to be successful?
- Will you represent the organization professionally?
- Are you suited to the position and will you fit in with the rest of the department?
- Are you personable and pleasant to be around?
- Do you project an aura of excitement and enthusiasm for the position and the company?
- Will you last at the job—are your career goals in line with the job and the organization?

You also have goals:

- You will want to determine your level of interest in the company and the position they are offering.
- You'll want to convince the interviewer you understand the requirements of the position and are exactly what the firm needs in terms of skills, experience, and personality.

- You'll want to highlight your key skills and validate them with your memorable examples.
- You will want to demonstrate your sincerity, your professionalism, and your enthusiasm.
- You'll want to get the offer—that way *you* are in the driver's seat and the choice of whether or not to accept the position is *yours*.

The basic 5-part interview format

1. **Icebreaker:** This is the initial small talk that takes place when you first walk through the door. Although your interaction is chatty, this is your all-important first impression. Much of the underlying communication is nonverbal, so watch your posture, give a firm handshake, keep your body language open (no crossed arms), make eye contact, and smile. Show you are confident, courteous, friendly, and at ease with yourself and the situation. Even though the talk may be "small," the first couple of minutes are likely to be decisive. Many psychologists suggest people make up their minds about someone within the first few minutes of meeting them.

2. **Background probe:** Most interviewers will begin the formal part of the interview with an open-ended question to get you talking about yourself and your background. Most commonly, they'll say something like: "Tell me about yourself," or "Give me a little about your background," or ask, "What brings you here today?"

   Although the above background probe examples may appear to be very different, they can each be answered using the same response. Any ideas? Of course, you've got it! This is the perfect opportunity to give the interviewer a rendition of your catchy commercial/branding statement targeted to the position for which you're applying. In general, your response should include your level of experience, key skills relating to the job, any required education, and, as appropriate, a couple of key accomplishments. (You'll see an example of this shortly under "Questions to Anticipate: Tell me about yourself.")

3. **Work history/resume review:** This is your chance to tell your story. You will need to explain your skills, abilities, accomplishments, and career goals and back these up with examples of you performing your work at its best. Emphasize your added value and set yourself apart from the competition. Use noteworthy examples whereby you: increased sales, reduced costs, saved time, improved quality, led the team, came up with a new idea, turned a project around, etc.

   Be sure to stress your ability and willingness to perform at a high level and your interest in the position and the company. You can underscore your fit by using phrases such as: "In a position like this, I would draw upon my ability to..." or "In a company such as yours, I could use my experience in widget sales to..."

4. **Your questions:** The interviewer will ask if you have any questions for him/her regarding the position or the organization. Of course you do! And they are well thought out and prepared ahead of time. If you don't have questions, you will seem disinterested and unprofessional. (There are sample questions coming along in a minute, so let's carry on, shall we?)

5. **The close:** The interviewer draws the interview to a close and generally says something like: "We'll be in touch with you when we make a decision." But don't leave it at that! You will need to respond with a strong close of your own by saying "Now that we've had this conversation, I'm even more interested in the position. Can you tell me where you are in the hiring process?"

We'll go into more depth about the various components of the interview later in the chapter. Right now let's take a look at...

Other types of interviews

The screening interview: This interview is conducted over the phone. It's usually performed by a human resources representative or, in smaller organizations, by an assistant. The purpose of the screening interview is to weed out unqualified candidates. Questions are most frequently of a general nature regarding basic skills and experience.

Also, questions about salary are often asked: "What are your salary requirements?" and "What were you making at your last job?" are common. Job search specialists suggest deferring your response and, whenever possible, you'll want to do so. Keeping this information to yourself gives you the most leverage to negotiate should they offer you the position. You might say, "Right now I'm flexible. I'd like to find out more details about the job before discussing salary," or "Salary is important, but it's only part of the compensation package. I'd need to know more about general compensation before suggesting an income amount." And you can add, "But, as long as you brought the subject up, can you give me the range for the position?" That way you'll have the all-important salary information and the advantage when it comes time to negotiate.

Many times, however, the screener will insist you give her/him a salary number and you don't want to antagonize your interviewer during this initial conversation. If pressed, you can give your salary requirements in a range, i.e., low 70s, mid 70s, high 70s. This way you're providing a response but not pinning yourself down too much.

Coworker interviews: Most potential coworkers will be assessing how well you will fit within their team. Of course, they'll want to know that you have the skills to do the job, but much of their focus will be on personality. Be friendly, helpful, and enthusiastic. Show them you are a cooperative team player and someone they can count on to pull your own weight.

The group interview: From time-to-time you may find yourself interviewing before a group. Be sure to make frequent eye contact with everyone in the room, get each of their business cards so you can follow up with each one individually, and shake hands with everyone involved. Be as inclusive as possible and connect in a personal way with each participant.

Do your research!

A vital component to successful interviewing is preparation—research is the key!

Be certain to get a copy of the job description.
This is your primary way to be able to focus your responses and establish the fact that you are *the* candidate of choice. Create memorable examples that clearly and concisely suggest ways the organization would benefit from hiring *YOU*. Ask yourself: What problems can I solve? In which areas will my skills prove beneficial? How can I make a difference? What is the added value I can bring to this position? Why am I the #1 person for this job?

Research the company online and through your network. Pay special attention to recent press reports, management changes, and industry developments—locally, nationally, and internationally.

Find out what you can about the hiring manager and his/her needs. You can often acquire this information through your personal network. And, if you're working through a recruiter, ask him or her for any and all information on the company, position, and manager prior to an interview. Recruiters are paid on their ability to screen and promote only qualified candidates, so they'll want you to succeed. Therefore, they should be forthcoming with the information you will want to know.

Questions to anticipate

The following are a list of questions that are frequently asked in job interviews. Each question has a suggested response. However, as with everything else in a job search, one size does not fit all! Consider how *YOU* wish to respond, jot down some notes, and practice. If you really want to ensure you remember your desired responses (even while under the somewhat stressful circumstances of a job interview), record them. Then play them back as frequently as possible—while driving in your car or cleaning the house.

> **Tell me about yourself. *(Background probe)***
> *Answer with your branding statement targeted to the position. Your response to the initial background probe is important because it can set the tone for the entire interview. If you mention a particular achievement, the interviewer is likely to ask you to elaborate and you can structure the conversation to highlight the strengths and accomplishments you wish.*

"I'm a senior human resources professional with over fifteen years of experience in the high tech industry. Much of my background has been in employee development and training where I've used my project management and staff development skills to improve organizational performance. I spearheaded an initiative at Software Company X where I analyzed existing operations in the marketing department, oversaw training programs, and implemented strategies and procedures that improved performance by fifteen percent within a six-month period."

Why did you leave your last position?
Answer this one briefly, unemotionally and, if you were laid off, show you were part of a group. End your response on a positive note:

"I enjoyed my time at ABC organization and grew a lot in the position. However, due to the recent downturn in the economy, they were forced to cut staff and I was one out of 250 employees to leave. Now I'm looking forward to my next opportunity and am interested to find out more about the position you are offering here."

What makes you the right person for the job?
Match your skill set with the requirements listed in the posting and substantiate them with a strong example(s) demonstrating your abilities and experience.

"You're looking for an administrative assistant who can work for multiple managers, juggle a lot of balls simultaneously, and thrive in a fast-paced environment. In my most recent position, I reported to three high-level executives and had to frequently stop a project to send an urgent message to one of our most valued customers. I learned to prioritize my tasks and use my time so well that I had built-in allowances for these types of critical requests. I don't have a problem working under pressure... in fact, I tend to do very well in just these types of situations."

Why do you want to work here?
Start your response to this question with: "Well, I've done my homework..." (This shows you took the time to research the company and

that you're coming to the interview well prepared—a true plus that will impress the interviewer.)

"I've done my homework on XYZ Company and like what I see. I'm particularly impressed by your mission statement, your efforts to go green, and the high customer satisfaction rating you've achieved."

Tell me about your strengths.
Name several of your personal/professional traits relating to the job and substantiate them with an example(s).

"I'm detail-oriented, thorough, conscientious, and a team player. I've often been told *(speech softener if it makes you feel more comfortable)* that I can be counted on to get the job done on time and within budget. And I pride myself on my abilities to monitor workflow, prioritize effectively, delegate as needed, and oversee and track costs. My projects do come in on time and I've often saved the company more than fifteen percent in expenditures."

What would your last manager want us to know about you?
This is your chance to show additional strengths. Don't forget to substantiate them with a strong example(s) of you performing your work at its best.

"My manager would probably tell you I'm able to see the big picture and often come up with ideas nobody had previously considered. For example, our team was working on a project but things were bogging down—we weren't getting the buy-in from upper management we needed. So I came up with the suggestion that we conduct a needs assessment and pose certain questions to upper level managers to see where their true needs lie. We did this, gathered some extremely valuable information, and refocused our project to address the managers' input. The result was that our efforts proved a resounding success. Managers as well as employees were pleased at how we were able to streamline the manufacturing process, reduce time to market by ten percent, and eliminate the majority of product returns."

What were your three top accomplishments in your last position?
Prepare for this question by having several strong examples ready to go.

Do you work well under pressure?
Your answer, of course, will be "yes," unless you truly do wilt under pressure. If that is the case and they ask this question, it is probably a red flag indicating you will not do well in this job. At a minimum, it won't be a job you will love.

If "yes" is your answer, you'll need to back this up with an example to validate what you are saying about yourself.

What would differentiate you from other candidates I might interview?
This is another opportunity to show strengths, fit for the position, and added value. Remember to back up your claims with that all-important example(s).

What are your weaknesses?
You'll need to prepare for this question. Of course, we all have weaknesses but we want to present them in a way that won't hurt our chances for the job. Be sure and name something that is true for you but that only represents a small part of your work. As a counselor, if I said my weakness was my dislike for working closely with people—that certainly wouldn't bode well for my future prospects!

Another way of describing a weakness in a way that won't eliminate you is to put it in the past tense. Be sure and let the interviewer know you're aware of your weakness and have learned from your previous mistakes.

"When I first started career counseling, I got so involved with helping my clients, that I sometimes neglected to do the necessary paperwork after their session had ended. Once I was supposed to follow-up with a client and forgot because I hadn't made the proper notations. She got upset with me and, from then on, I've learned the importance of maintaining my records and giving myself the necessary follow-up reminders."

Watch using the weakness described in many books on interviewing: "I just work too hard and am too conscientious for my own good." Yeah, right!

Is there anything else I should know about you that I haven't yet asked?
This is another question you'll want to prepare for, as many interviewers will pose it at the end of the interview. However, it provides a great opportunity for you to do a last minute sales job highlighting YOU and stressing your fit for the position. Have a significant example ready for a strong close.

Nail the age-related questions

What do you plan to be doing in five years?
This question is asking about your career goals and it can be particularly difficult for older applicants because you may well want to be retired in five years. However that would not be your wisest choice of answers—no humorous replies about rocking chairs, golf, or sitting on the beach holding a drink garnished with little, colorful umbrellas. I always suggest that applicants "think politician!" Be positive and vague at the same time and say something like:

"I like what I do and think I'm good at it. And I'm sure a position such as this would provide me with many enjoyable challenges and chances for growth. I look forward to enlarging my skill set and taking advantage of any career opportunities that come my way."
(Grow with the company and grow with the position are the best types of answers to this question.)

Aren't you overqualified for the position?
Actually this question is asked far less frequently than you might think. You've already been screened as to your suitability for the position by your resume. So, if this comes up during an interview, it may be a signal that someone on the hiring team may be feeling threatened by you. It's best to respond to this question in a positive and vague manner, much like the suggestion above.

"My work gives me great satisfaction. I'm certain working in a firm such as this will afford me many exciting challenges and opportunities for growth. Each organization is different and I look forward to learning new ways of doing my job and acting as a supportive member of your team."

If, in fact, you've decided to step down a bit and take a job with less responsibility, you can say something like:

"I've enjoyed my role as a manager but have come to the realization that I prefer doing the hands-on work myself. I get a real boost by seeing a tangible result from my efforts, so this position should be a perfect fit for me and my current career path."

Behavioral style interview questions

About twenty years ago, a new style of interviewing became all the rage. Interviewers were aware that applicants could anticipate certain questions would be asked of them and, therefore, prepare their answers ahead of time. So they came up with the idea of asking event-specific questions. These often begin with "tell me about a time when you..." or "what would you do if..."

Can you really prepare for event-specific, behavioral style interviewing? Actually, the answer is a resounding "yes," and I strongly suggest that you do.

First review the job requirements in light of the types of behavioral questions interviewers are likely to pose. For example, if your responsibilities include leading a team, then you'll probably be asked about your leadership style. In this case you'll want to create noteworthy examples that display your leadership skills: motivating reluctant team members, building a cohesive team, monitoring performance, giving necessary feedback, etc.

For her interview, our salesperson would come up with examples showing how she turned around a reluctant buyer, closed a major deal, made her presence known in a new territory, actively built her client base, etc.

But what if the salesperson were asked to give an example of how she took a client away from the competition? This is an important question. However our salesperson friend doesn't recall an example of when she did this. Not a problem! Should this happen, she (and you) can say something like:

"Nothing specific to your question comes to mind, but I can give you an example of a similar situation where I showed initiative." Then give the interviewer an example you've already prepared.

Remember, it's often helpful to "think politician" when you are at an interview. Positive, targeted responses will generally work—you're answering their questions, but you're adjusting your answers to cover the experience you're choosing to highlight.

Think politician!

Questions for you to ask

Ideally you'll want to take a conversational approach to interviewing, get to know the interviewer, and ascertain his or her needs prior to trying to sell yourself in an interview. Remember what we learned in Strategy Two: Every employer is looking for the same thing—a problem solver. But you can't present yourself as the problem solver of their dreams without a thorough understanding of the specifics.

Of course you've familiarized yourself with the position description, but many of the hiring manager's true needs may not be listed. So you'll want to assume the role of consultant, not simply a jobseeker, and ask how you can make the hiring manager's life easier. You can do this by taking the initiative with a question-answer-question approach. Answer the question that was asked and follow up with related question of your own.

Interviewer: "Tell me about yourself."

You: Present your branding statement followed by, "Now that I've told you about my background, can you tell me what you see to be the most pressing aspects of the position?"

—or—

Interviewer: "This job demands a certain amount of oversight. How do you handle authority?"

You: "I handle authority just fine but, since you brought it up, can you tell me a little about your management style and the expectations for the position?"

Using the question-answer-question format, the interview becomes more of a conversation between equals and, many times, you can even help the hiring manager clarify and verbalize his/her true requirements.

You: "If I'm understanding you correctly, you're looking for someone who can oversee and schedule existing volunteers, but you're really most interested in someone who's effective at recruiting new ones into the organization."

Interviewer: "Yes, I guess that's right."

You: "When I was the volunteer coordinator at the Nonprofit 123, I was responsible for managing all aspects of the volunteers' work with our recipients. But I was most known for my ability to perform community outreach. I was a regular speaker at community organizations, Rotary Clubs, church groups, and the like, and I designed and produced a variety of brochures and leaflets explaining our work. As a result, I was able to double our volunteer staff within the first year I held the position."

Because people hire to fulfill their own needs, you won't "talk" them into hiring you, you'll "listen" them into hiring you. Ask the right questions, find out their problems, and present yourself as *the problem solver* they've been waiting for.

Sample questions to get the interviewer talking:

- What are the most pressing components of the job?
- What needs to get done in the first three months?
- What do you view to be the long-range goals for the position?
- How can the new person make your job easier?
- How would you like someone in this position to handle situation X?
- As the manager, which characteristics are most important to you for an employee to be successful?

Other questions you'll want to ask

There are several additional questions you may want to pose to the interviewer. These may deal with the company, the department, his or her expectations, or the actual position.

- Is this a newly created position? If so, why?
- How will the new hire's success be measured?
- What type of training will the new hire receive?
- What do you like most about working here?
- How much travel is expected?

So now let's pull it all together and get you prepared to knock 'em dead at your next interview!

Prepare in detail

Get yourself psyched to win! Even though playing up your strengths may not come naturally to you, it's expected at an interview. This is not the time to be shy. You don't want to come across as a braggart, but you do want to display an inner confidence in your skills and abilities. So, if needed, get comfortable telling your "story" by doing a mock interview with a sympathetic friend. Overcoming your reluctance to speak highly of yourself is essential if you hope to convince an employer to hire *YOU*. Here's a brief review of what you'll need to do:

- Review the posting in great detail and demonstrate how your experience fits with the requirements for the job.
- Research the company and find out (if possible) the hiring manager's needs.
- Practice your answers to the most frequently asked questions in light of the position requirements and the needs of the hiring manager/company. For additional general questions and suggested answers, turn to the Internet. Enter "sample interview questions" into your search engine and you'll find several pages of listings. (Again, you may want to record your answers so that you can hear your responses over and over.)
- Anticipate any objections and be able to speak to these as well as to your strengths.
- Be able to highlight your skills in each of the three areas:
    - Knowledge based, technical skills: how will your educational background, training, and specific technical skills benefit the organization?
    - Personal traits and skill sets: how does your personal style, work ethic, ability to get along with others, etc. create added value?
    - Transferable skills: how will the skills you've learned in previous positions help you succeed and contribute to the goals of the new job?

- Create a minimum of ten memorable examples to show how you've achieved results in your previous positions. (These should be in addition to examples on your resume so they can answer behavioral style interview questions.)
- If desired, do a dry run. Drive by the company a couple of days ahead of time about the same time of day as your actual interview. That way you'll know the route and be able to anticipate the traffic patterns you're likely to face.

What to bring to the interview:

- A professional looking portfolio (the kind with a pad of paper on one side and a pocket on the other.) Taking brief notes during the interview demonstrates organization and interest in the job. It also gives you something to do with your hands so you don't inadvertently cross your arms.
- Information on the company and contact numbers. In case there's an accident or some other delay and you're running late, you can call to let them know.
- Several copies of your resume to hand out to interviewers. You would be surprised at the number of interviewers who are unprepared and may not even have seen your resume. This way you can hand them a clean copy that's neatly printed on cotton bond paper.
- Special Strategy: create a copy of your resume for yourself! After you open up your portfolio, have it available for you to refer to quickly and easily. During the questioning, it's fine for you to glance down from time to time. But here's the super secret—write keywords in the margin of your resume that will jog your memory as to the examples you've prepared. This way, even if you get a bit nervous and your mind goes temporarily blank, you've got the answers in front of you! Your "cheat sheet" will help you feel better prepared and much more relaxed.
- Your list of questions about the position and the company.
- A calendar/BlackBerry in case they want to schedule additional interviews.

Dress for success

Most everywhere we turn these days, the world has gotten more casual. And, yes, this may likely be true for your interview outfit as well. You don't want to overdress too much because clothing is a nonverbal message that you fit with the position and the environment. (If you were interviewing for a job as a clerk in a copy shop, you'd look out of place wearing a black suit.) However, you do want to show that you realize this is a special occasion and dress accordingly.

Here are some rules of thumb:

- Dress for the job you are going for, but take it up a notch. In other words, if your position is very casual and you'll be wearing jeans for the most part, wear a pair of cotton or wool slacks.
- Even if you're dressing casually for an interview, a jacket is always a good idea. It shows a certain amount of professionalism and projects an aura of confidence.
- Wear conservative jewelry and accessorize accordingly—same with makeup.
- Make certain that your outfit is clean and pressed and your shoes are polished.
- Be sure to wear your very best asset—a warm, friendly smile!

Blast away the stereotypes that sting!

Remember the stereotypes we identified in the Introduction—those less-than-stellar generalizations younger people may hold against us? If not, here's a recap:

- We're tired, slow, and unenthusiastic
- We're not technologically savvy
- We're set in our ways and don't want to try new things
- We won't want to report to a younger boss
- We're just putting in our time until retirement
- We're too expensive

Most of these nasty stereotypes can be dispelled through your nonverbal messages. Energy and enthusiasm are two that come to mind. Other points to remember that will go a long way are:

- Present a youthful appearance. Make certain your outfit is stylish, your glasses are contemporary, and, if necessary, whiten your teeth. If gray hair is not your friend, consider coloring it.
- Project energy and confidence through your posture, handshake, eye contact, voice, and smile.
- Let them know you've kept up to date professionally and technology is not a problem for you. (If it is—take a class! You don't want something that might be easily remedied holding you back.)
- Give several examples of how you're a quick study and enjoy learning new things. Periodically refer to the fact that you enjoy your work, feel you're good at it, and want to continue to grow your skill set.
- Proactively state you enjoy working with and learning from people of all ages. You've reported to younger bosses in the past and it was never a problem.
- You won't want to discuss salary in early interview sessions but, when the time is right and you feel comfortable doing so, be certain to let them know you're flexible. There are many factors that fall under compensation and salary might not be your main concern at this point.

End on a high note!

Many times interviewers will conclude the session saying something like: " Thank you for coming in. We have several other people we'll be interviewing and we will be letting you know shortly."

That's all well and good, but you want to end on a high note. Make certain the interviewer is aware of your enthusiasm for the position and the organization by responding with something along the lines of: "Now that we've had this conversation, I'm even more interested in the position. Can you tell me where you are on the hiring process?" Or, " Can you give me the next steps?" And, if you're feeling especially assertive or the interview has warranted it, you might even end with: "If I have any additional questions, might I contact you?" This leaves the door open to a follow-up phone call or e-mail.

You want to leave your interviewer with the knowledge you *care* about the position. Managers want people on their team who wish to be there. They want someone to be skilled enough to solve their problems but they especially want someone who will be a problem solver with a smile on their face. So don't be shy about letting them know you'd love to become a part of their team. A bit of enthusiasm and a good, strong close will go a long, long way!

Follow up with a thank you note.

Be certain to do this, as many interviewers will view the absence of a thank you note or e-mail as a sign that you don't care about the job. Refer to our example under Strategy Seven.

A thoughtful thank you is the perfect follow-up!

STRATEGY EIGHT: ACTION STEPS

Create your own responses to frequently asked questions ~

Tell me about yourself.

____

____

____

____

____

____

____

Why did you leave your last position?

____

____

____

____

____

____

____

What makes you the right person for the job?

Why do you want to work here?

Tell me about your strengths.

____

____

____

____

____

____

____

____

What would your last manager want us to know about you?

____

____

____

____

____

____

____

____

What were your three top accomplishments in your last position?

Do you work well under pressure?

What would differentiate you from other candidates I might interview?

____

____

____

____

____

____

____

____

What do you plan to be doing in five years?

____

____

____

____

____

____

____

____

Aren't you overqualified for this position?

____

____

____

____

____

____

____

____

Is there anything else I should know about you that I haven't asked?

____

____

____

____

____

____

____

____

What are your weaknesses?

____

____

____

____

Create 10 memorable examples (in addition to those on your resume) that can be used to respond to behavioral style interview questions. Highlight the skills and personality traits your desired position requires, e.g., leadership, follow-through, team-building, people skills, using initiative, creative problem solving, etc. Having these examples ready is essential to being well prepared because event-specific, behavioral style questions are becoming the norm in many interviews.

Example 1

____

____

____

____

____

____

____

____

Example 2

Example 3

Example 4

Example 5

Example 6

Example 7

Example 8

Example 9

Example 10

Which questions will you be asking?

____

____

____

____

____

____

____

____

____

____

____

You've done it! You've wowed them with your interview and now they want your references…

STRATEGY NINE: MAKE YOUR REFERENCES ZING

As we covered earlier, many employers are turning to LinkedIn and other social networking sites as a substitute for more formal references. Thus, be mindful about what you put out on the Internet so that it doesn't come back to bite you!

The idea of formal references, however, is not dead and these can prove extremely helpful to landing you the job you will love.

There are a few simple guidelines to use when dealing with references:

- Ask them. This seems like a basic first step but many people overlook it and provide names of people on the assumption that they will give a positive reference. Do not do this! Even if your reference may have wanted to give you a good recommendation, they will be surprised by the call and, therefore, unprepared.
- Tell your references what you're looking to do and give them a copy of your resume. This is also an opportunity to ask for feedback on your resume from someone who knows your work.
- Try to get references from different levels within the organization: your manager or supervisor, peers and coworkers and, if you managed subordinates, their names as well. That way the interviewer will get 360-degree feedback.
- You only need to provide three to five names. However, you can ask several people to act as a reference for you and then "cherry-pick" the most appropriate references for specific positions.

- Remember these are *professional* references who can speak to your performance at work. Although community leaders and other prominent individuals may be well known, unless they have a direct relationship with what you do, it's best to omit them from your list.
- Do not give out names of references until the job offer looks promising. If your references have already been contacted several times, they are not as likely to be as glowing about your skills and experience as they might have been on the first call or two.
- Don't expect to get all the references you might like. Many organizations discourage employees from providing references because they are concerned about repercussions and potential lawsuits. Sometimes you'll be unable get references from your most recent place of employment. However, don't worry. Simply let your interviewer know about the company policy. He/she will understand your situation as disallowing references is now a widespread practice.
- Once you've made it through the interview process and to the point that a company wants to check your references, alert them and let them know that they are about to be contacted.
- Tell them some of the major points the interviewer covered regarding his/her needs and how you responded to these. Then you can suggest that they speak to three or four of your strongest accomplishments. (Remember you already gave them your resume so they know how you're marketing yourself.) This way you'll make it easy for them because they'll know how to respond, and you'll get the reference you want! You might say something like:

  > *"Thanks again for offering to provide a reference for me. The hiring manager seemed especially interested in my ability to handle difficult prospects, turn them around, and close the deal. Could you tell them about the time I met with the CEO of XYZ*

Company and was able to get him to reverse his opinion? If you recall, we brought in over $50,000 worth of business on that one, and I know the hiring manager would want your perspective on how I accomplished that."

- The same idea holds true for letters of reference. Rather than just asking someone to write a letter of reference, either write one yourself or provide an outline and several points to cover. Again, you've made it much easier for your reference and you've targeted the letter to the strengths you wish to highlight.
- Remember to thank your references and let them know when you land a job.

I've had my ups and downs but I made it!

STRATEGY NINE: ACTION STEPS

Prepare your list of references ~

- Put your complete contact information at the top of the page. Many people submit a list with only the word "references" at the top. This can easily be separated from your additional information and then your carefully selected references would be rendered useless.
- Don't forget to ask references from coworkers within various levels of your organization: managers, peers, employees who reported to you.
- Add a line that shows the relationship you had with your reference, e.g., "former manager."

References template:

Name and title: ____________________________________

Company: ____

Reference's contact information: _________________________________
(phone, e-mail)

Relationship to applicant: _______________________________________

Name and title: ____________________________________

Company: ____

Reference's contact information: _________________________________
(phone, e-mail)

Relationship to applicant: _______________________________________

Name and title: ________________________________

Company: ____________________________________

Reference's contact information: _____________________________
(phone, e-mail)

Relationship to applicant: ___________________________________

Name and title: ________________________________

Company: ____________________________________

Reference's contact information: _____________________________
(phone, e-mail)

Relationship to applicant: ___________________________________

Name and title: ________________________________

Company: ____________________________________

Reference's contact information: _____________________________
(phone, e-mail)

Relationship to applicant: ___________________________________

You're almost there! Now it's time to cover your final strategy…

STRATEGY TEN: NEGOTIATE THE DEAL WITH FINESSE

The goal of any negotiation is not necessarily to get as much money as you can. You'll want to get hired and work at a job and an organization you love, so you'll want everyone concerned to feel that the deal was a win/win situation. If you push for the top salary, you'd better be very certain of your ability to perform. They won't be allowing you much of a learning curve if you're starting at the top. On the other hand, you don't want to feel like you were cheated either. Raises are generally based on current salary so, if you come in too low, you'll likely be paying for that mistake for years.

Make sure you have a plan

- Know your salary requirements based on your own desire and your worth in the current market.
    - Sources of information include: recruiters, state board of labor statistics, professional journals, competitive organizations, networking meetings and interviews, Salary.com, SimplyHired.com, and Google to name a few.
    - If your experience warrants it, you can take the industry range and add 10 to15 percent to start the negotiation process.

- Consider other compensation items to negotiate:
    - Bonus (sign on, performance, etc.)
    - Early performance review
    - Stock/stock options
    - Profit sharing
    - Pension/annuity plans

- Health benefits
- Education/additional training
- Car/car allowance
- Vacation/comp time
- Professional/social memberships

- Consider task/job-related items to negotiate:
    - Title/position
    - Authority/decision-making responsibilities
    - Additional staff
    - Budgets
    - Resources/equipment

Negotiate like a pro!

- Negotiate and define task items first. You'll want to be very clear on the breadth of your responsibilities and what will be expected of you.
- If possible, have them state the salary range first and come in with a response that's close to the top of that range if you feel comfortable doing so. You can always negotiate down—it's far more difficult to negotiate up!
- Remember the interviewer has made you the offer and thinks you are the best person for the job. This may be the only time in your relationship when you hold the advantage.
- Also remember you will often be dealing and negotiating with your future boss, so you'll want to be sure to create a win/win situation.
- Generally, you won't want to accept an offer immediately. It's usually best to take a day or two to "sleep on it." Show enthusiasm, thank the interviewer for the offer, and say you will get back to him or her shortly.
- Get the offer in writing with the compensation package, any additional benefits, and the job description clearly defined. If you are negotiating with a small firm and they

don't usually provide written offers, you can suggest you want to make sure that everything is clear from all sides and would be happy to write up the offer as you understand it. It is *always* better to have things clearly defined and in writing!

Refer to the exercises you completed in Part I of this book

- Take some time to review your values, motivated skills, and preferred work environment.
- How likely will this position fit with your career needs and goals?
- Will this truly be a job you will love? If not, and you need an income, take it but continue looking for something more suitable.
- Remember all of the strengths, skills, and experience you bring with you and don't settle for something you don't want!

This is an important decision—make sure you have all your ducks in a row!

STRATEGY TEN: ACTION STEPS

To clearly identify your priorities, determine the importance of the following and place them in rank order from one to ten ~

________ Position description and responsibilities

________ Job title

________ Base salary

________ Early performance review with potential merit-based raise

________ Health care benefits

________ Pension/retirement plans

________ Training opportunities

________ Vacation/personal days

________ Telecommuting/flex time/job share

________ Other

And now for some final thoughts....

YOU GOT THE JOB—HERE'S YOUR FINAL TIP

TAKE TIME TO CELEBRATE!

Whether you take a vacation before your start, a weekend getaway, or just a night out on the town, be sure to mark this momentous occasion with a worthy celebration. You've worked hard to achieve your new position, weathered many ups and downs, pushed your personal boundaries, and come out the winner!

Be certain to also alert and thank your network of friends and supporters. A brief message letting them know that you've landed a job and where you'll be working, along with a note of gratitude for all of their help will be much appreciated. Also, as job security is a thing of the past, it's always to your benefit to keep your network active.

Something to consider

By the time you've reached your fiftieth birthday, you've lived 18,250 days on the planet! You're a richer and more accomplished person for it, and you have a lot to offer your new employer. Through your efforts, you've achieved a fresh start with new challenges and opportunities for growth. Like we used to say back in the good old days: *Today is the first day of the rest of your life*. So breathe in and feel the glow of your accomplishment—it truly is a time to celebrate new beginnings...

And let me be the first to offer my congratulations on successfully landing the job you love!

Made in the USA
Lexington, KY
27 January 2012